1. Robert V. Whitlow

2. Buck Shaw

3. Ben Martin

6. Fisher DeBerry

4. Bill Parcells

5. Ken Hatfield

7. Troy Calhoun

The United States Army Air Corps (USAAC) was the statutory forerunner of the United States Air Force. Renamed from the Air Service on 2 July 1926, it was part of the United States Army and the immediate predecessor of the United States Army Air Forces (USAAF), established on June 20, 1941.

Great Coaches
In
Air Force Football

From the beginning of football all the way to Coach Calhoun's latest team

You'll love the great stories about the great football coaches beginning fort with the Air Force Academy's founding in 1954 just 65 years ago. After discussing the official founding of the Academy on April 1, 1954, by Harold E. Talbott, the book takes us on a ride in time from when Air Force played freshman teams to the many great years of Fisher DeBerry and Troy Calhoun.

When Air Force came into being, the football team was immediately a competitor for the Commander in Chief's Trophy, even before the Trophy were conceived. Air Force won is very first game and that was a great omen for the future.

Not only is AFA a non-push-over for Army and Navy, they lead the Trophy series. Air Force is tops in three-way competition football trophies with 20; Navy 15; and Army 8. The Air Force football winning tradition lives on today under Head Coach Troy Calhoun.

You will learn that like no other football team, the US Air Force Falcons are fierce and passionate competitors. From the stadium to the classroom to the research lab, the US Air Force Falcons always play to win.

You will learn that Air Force's first official football game was in 1955 long after the rules of American football had been completely defined. Under coach Robert V. Whitlow, in his only year as Head Coach, they won their first game v the Denver University Freshmen 34-18. In this first season, with a record of 4-4 they first beat the Denver University Freshmen 34-18. When the Falcons began to play all varsity squads in year 3, under Coach Buck Shaw. the Falcons achieved their first winning record of 6-2-1. Three years later in 1959, they tied Army 13-13 in their first game against another service academy. Go Air Force

On Sept 8, 1954, the year before the Falcons football program began, it was coach Lt. Col (later full Colonel) Robert Winslow who was appointed the first Director of Athletics for the Air Force Academy. The following year, he became the first head football coach. Thus, in more ways than one, he is responsible for football being played at the Academy along with other sports such as basketball, baseball, indoor track, outdoor track, ice hockey, wrestling, soccer, swimming, tennis, gymnastics, golf, rifle, pistol, and skiing. So far, since 1955, the Air Force has played over 730 games with a w/l/t record of 394–331–13.

This book moves quickly through the coaches after Buck Shaw through immortals such as Ben Martin, Bill Parcells, Ken Hatfield, Fisher DeBerry, and the book wraps up with a full-treatment of today's outstanding coach, Troy Calhoun. This book highlights each coach and shows the record of each coach in each of their seasons.

This book is your finest source for a great read on your favorite service academy college football team (Air Force's Falcons) and its outstanding coaches. It is the closest thing to an all-encompassing, full-blown Air Force football encyclopedia about Falcons coaching—a blow by blow history with tales of the great coaching moments. This book is for your reading pleasure, but it also can be a great reference tool for you when you want to see how a particular Air Force football coach did in any year since 1955.

If you are an Air Force Football fan. you will not want to put this book down.

Brian Kelly

Copyright © February 2019, Brian W. Kelly Editor: Brian P. Kelly
Title: Great Coaches in Air Force Football Author Brian Kelly

All rights reserved: No part of this book may be reproduced or transmitted in any form, or by any means, electronic or mechanical, including photocopying, recording, scanning, faxing, or by any information storage and retrieval system, without permission from the publisher, LETS GO PUBLISH, in writing.

Disclaimer: Though judicious care was taken throughout the writing and the publication of this work that the information contained herein is accurate, there is no expressed or implied warranty that all information in this book is 100% correct. Therefore, neither LETS GO PUBLISH, nor the author accepts liability for any use of this work.

Trademarks: A number of products and names referenced in this book are trade names and trademarks of their respective companies.

Referenced Material: *Standard Disclaimer: The information in this book has been obtained through personal and third-party observations, interviews, and copious research. Where unique information has been provided, or extracted from other sources, those sources are acknowledged within the text of the book itself or in the References area in the front matter. Thus, there are no formal footnotes nor is there a bibliography section. Any picture that does not have a source was taken from various sites on the Internet with no credit attached. If resource owners would like credit in the next printing, please email publisher.*

Published by: ....LETS GO PUBLISH!
Editor in Chief ....Brian P. Kelly
Email: ....info@letsgopublish.com
Web site .... www.letsgopublish.com

Library of Congress Copyright Information Pending
Book Cover Design by **Brian Kelly**
Editor—Brian P. Kelly

ISBN Information: The International Standard Book Number (ISBN) is a unique machine-readable identification number, which marks any book unmistakably. The ISBN is the clear standard in the book industry. 159 countries and territories are officially ISBN members. The Official ISBN for this book is

978-1-947402-75-1

The price for this work is:........... $ 12.95 USD

10   9   8   7   6   5   4   3   2   1

Air Force Football Seasons by Year/Coach.

YEAR	Falcons Coach	Record	Conference Record
1955	Robert V. Whitlow	4–4–0	
1956	Buck Shaw	6–2–1	
1957	Buck Shaw	3–6–1	
1958	Ben Martin	9–0–2	
1959	Ben Martin	5–4–1	
1960	Ben Martin	4–6	
1961	Ben Martin	3–7	
1962	Ben Martin	5–5	
1963	Ben Martin	7–4	
1964	Ben Martin	4–5–1	
1965	Ben Martin	3–6–1	
1966	Ben Martin	4–6	
1967	Ben Martin	2–6–2	
1968	Ben Martin	7–3	
1969	Ben Martin	6–4	
1970	Ben Martin	9–3	
1971	Ben Martin	6–4	
1972	Ben Martin	6–4	
1973	Ben Martin	6–4	
1974	Ben Martin	2–9	
1975	Ben Martin	2–8–1	
1976	Ben Martin	4–7	
1977	Ben Martin	2–8–1	
1978	Bill Parcells	3–8	*Conference*
1979	Ken Hatfield	2–9	*Record*
1980	Ken Hatfield	2–9–1	1–3
1981	Ken Hatfield	4–7	2–3
1982	Ken Hatfield	8–5	4–3
1983	Ken Hatfield	10–2	5–2
1984	Fisher DeBerry	8–4	4–3
1985	Fisher DeBerry	12–1	7–1
1986	Fisher DeBerry	6–5	5–2
1987	Fisher DeBerry	9–4	6–2
1988	Fisher DeBerry	5–7	3–5
1989	Fisher DeBerry	8–4–1	5–1–1
1990	Fisher DeBerry	7–5	3–4
1991	Fisher DeBerry	10–3	6–2
1992	Fisher DeBerry	7–5	4–4
1993	Fisher DeBerry	4–8	1–7
1994	Fisher DeBerry	8–4	6–2
1995	Fisher DeBerry	8–5	6–2
1996	Fisher DeBerry	6–5	5–3

YEAR	Falcons Coach	Record	Conference Record
1997	Fisher DeBerry	10–3	6–2
1998	Fisher DeBerry	12–1	7–1
1999	Fisher DeBerry	6–5	2–5
2000	Fisher DeBerry	9–3	5–2
2001	Fisher DeBerry	6–6	3–4
2002	Fisher DeBerry	8–5	4–3
2003	Fisher DeBerry	7–5	3–4
2004	Fisher DeBerry	5–6	3–4
2005	Fisher DeBerry	4–7	3–5
2006	Fisher DeBerry	4–8	3–4
2007	Troy Calhoun	9–4	6–2
2008	Troy Calhoun	8–5	5–3
2009	Troy Calhoun	8–5	5–3
2010	Troy Calhoun	9–4	5–3
2011	Troy Calhoun	7–6	3–4
2012	Troy Calhoun	6–7	5–3
2013	Troy Calhoun	2–10	0–8
2014	Troy Calhoun	10–3	5–3
2015	Troy Calhoun	8–6	6–2
2016	Troy Calhoun	10–3	5–3
2017	Troy Calhoun	5–7	4–4
2018	Troy Calhoun	5–7	3–5

Air Force played originally as an independent Team. In 1980, the team formally joined the Western Athletic Conference. In 1999, Air Force Moved to the Mountain West Conference.

Record (W-L-T): 384-325-12
Conferences: MWC, WAC, Ind
Conf. Championships: 3
Bowl Record: 26 Bowls, 12-13-1, .481 W-L%

Total Games 1,323

Seasons	62	
Total Wins	**384**	
Total Losses	**325**	
Total Ties	**12**	* Prior to Overtime Rules
Stats from	1967 through August 2019	

Acknowledgments:

I appreciate all the help that I received in putting this book together, along with the 194 other books from the past.

My printed acknowledgments were once so large that book readers needed to navigate too many pages to get to page one of the text. To permit me more flexibility, I put my acknowledgment list online at www.letsgopublish.com. The list of acknowledgments continues to grow. Believe it or not, it once cost about a dollar more to print each book.

Thank you all on the big list in the sky and God bless you all for your help.

Please check out www.letsgopublish.com to read the latest version of my heartfelt acknowledgments updated for this book. Thank you all!

In this book, I received some extra special help from many avid football friends including Dennis Grimes, Gerry Rodski, Wily Ky Eyely, Angel Brent Evans, Angel Irene McKeown Kelly, Angel Edward Joseph Kelly Sr., Angel Edward Joseph Kelly Jr., Ann Flannery, Angel James Flannery Sr., Mary Daniels, Bill Daniels, Robert Garry Daniels, Angel Sarah Janice Daniels, Angel Punkie Daniels, Joe Kelly and Diane Kelly. Another recent angel, always there to help is Jim Faller and of course the always impressive Theodore "O'Door" Szydlowski.

References

I learned how to write creatively in Grade School at St. Boniface. I even enjoyed reading some of my own stuff as a toddler.

At Meyers High School and King's College and Wilkes-University, I learned how to research, write bibliographies and footnote every non-original thought I might have ever had. I learned to hate ibid, and op. cit., and I hated assuring that I had all citations written down in the proper sequence. Having to pay attention to such details took my desire to write creatively and diminished it with busy work.

As a highly published author, I know it is necessary for the world to stop plagiarism so authors and publishers can get paid properly, but for an honest writer, it sure is annoying. I wrote many proposals while with IBM and whenever I needed to cite something, I cited it in place, because my readers, IT Managers, could care less about tracing the vagaries of citations and their varied formats.

I always hated to use stilted footnotes, or produce a lengthy, perfectly formatted bibliography. I bet most bibliographies are flawed because even the experts on such drivel do not like the tedium.

I wrote 194 books before this book and several hundred articles published by many magazines and newspapers and I only cite when an idea is not mine or when I am quoting, and again, I choose to cite in place, and the reader does not have to trace strange numbers through strange footnotes and back to bibliography elements that may not be readily accessible or available. Academicians knowing all the rules of citation are not my audience. In this book, if you are a lover of Air Force football, you are my intended group of readers

Yet, I would be kidding you, if in a book about the Great Moments in Air Force Football, I tried to bluff my way into trying to make you think that I knew everything before I began to write anything in this book. I spent as much time researching as writing. I might even call myself an expert of sorts now about the Air Force Falcons. This team literally is America's team. Though it is the third Service Academy to play College football, everybody in America has at one time watched and enjoyed Air Force Football, especially when the Falcons are having winning seasons, and more especially when the Air Force is beating either Army or Navy.

Without any pain on your part you can read this book from cover to cover to enjoy the stories about the many *Great Coaches in Air Force Football*.

It took me about two months to write this book. If I were to have made sure that a thought of mine was not a thought somebody else ever had, this book never would have been completed or the citations pages would more than likely exceed the prose. Everybody takes credit for everything in sports writing—at least that's what I have found.

I used the Air Force's 60th anniversary PDF to get many of the facts and summaries and recaps from whatever source I could to get the scores of all the games. I verified facts when possible. There is little opinion where facts are presented. There are many web sites that have great information and facts. Ironically most internet stories are the same exact stories. Who's got the original? While I was writing the book, I wrote down a bunch of Internet references and at one time, in other books such as this, I listed them right here en-masse in this section. They were the least read pages. No more. Unless I am citing a reference in a section of the book, you will not see the URL. I continually hunt for articles written by students to amplify the text I present.

While I was writing this book, because I was not sure that my citations within the text would be enough, and I was not producing a bibliography, I copied URLs into some of the book text in those cases in which I had read articles or had downloaded material and had brought articles or pieces of articles into this book. Hopefully, this will satisfy any request for additional citations. If there is anything, which needs a specific citation, I would be pleased to change the text. Just contact me. Your stuff is your stuff.

Many of the facts in this book are also put forth in the Air Force book 1956-2015, freely available on the Internet. Our thanks for the use of this material for the accurate production of this book. This, however, is a unique book as you will find. It is not a copy of anything.

This book is a great source about Air Force, football—where you can find a ton of information about your favorite Air Force teams.

Enjoy

Preface:

This book is all about the great coaches in Air Force Falcon football over the years. The Air Force Falcons have been ready to play every day once the season begins. This is because there have been seven great attentive coaches making sure the "boys," know how to get the job done.

The Falcon has been the official mascot of the United States Air Force Academy since almost the founding of the academy. This is commemorated with a statue shown on the prior page. It is mounted in front of Falcon Stadium in Colorado. The Falcon always points to the opponent's end zone.

In this book, along the way to today, we study the founding of the Air Force Academy. It is a military academy for officer cadets of the United States Air Force. Its campus is located in the western United States in Colorado, immediately north of Colorado Springs in El Paso County. Wikipedia. Its formal address is U.S. Air Force Academy, CO

Before the current coach, coach Trop Calhoun, there were six other fine coaches which are highlighted in this book. Fisher DeBerry was and still is the all-time leader in seasons coached at Air Force with twenty-three. Current AF Coach Calhoun has a lot of years to cover before he will overtake the great Fisher DeBerry for some very important stats such as games won. The Air Force likes Calhoun a lot and they have had only seven coaches in total since 1955 so nobody really knows what the future may hold.

Air Force is such a new team that they have no national championships to their credit, but the team never quits. At the 60th anniversary, a lot of stats were marshalled together for their tribute book. Some of these are as follows:

- Two (2) 12-win seasons (1985 and 1998)
- Two (2) Conference coaches of the year
- Four (4) Falcons have been selected to the College Football Hall of Fame
- Four (4) Falcons have been finalists for the Heisman Trophy
- Four (4) 4 straight wins over Notre Dame (1982-85)
- Seven (7) Head Coaches, including College Football Hall of Famer Fisher DeBerry
- Six seasons with 10 or more wins (83, 85, 91, 97, 98 and 14)
- Five (5) Consensus All-Americans (Brock Strom, 1958; Ernie Jennings, 1970; Scott Thomas, 1985, Chad Hennings, 1987; Carlton McDonald, 1992)
- Six (6) Falcons have played in NFL games
- Seven (7) Falcons drafted by the NFL
- Eleven (11) Players named conference player of the year a total of 14 times
- Twenty 20 Commander-in-Chief Trophy Titles
- Twenty (20) Trips to the White House. No other college or professional team has visited the White House more than the Air Force Falcons
- Twenty-Four (24) Bowl Games, including seven in the last eight years
- Twenty-five (25) Falcons have earned NCAA Postgraduate Scholarships
- Twenty-Eight (28) Conference Rushing Titles
- Thirty-one (31) Falcons have earned Academic All-America honors
- Thirty-Two (32) Falcons have earned All-America honors
- Sixty-one (61) percent of games won in Falcon Stadium
- Sixty-None (69) Falcons named first-team all-conference a total of 82 times.

With a list of plaudits bigger than your biggest arm, Air Force Football is here to stay and it is a seasoned sport at the Air Force Academy.

This book walks you through the whole Air Force football journey. We examine in detail all the coaches, and the successes from the early teams to today. This period began in 1955 with the first Air Force game against Denver University Freshmen W (34-18). Like all new teams, you can imagine the struggle of playing on a college football team when getting the right equipment was one of the biggest issues.

At the front of this book, you saw the 7 great Air Force coaches listed within the football seasons in which they coached--from season 1 in the 1955 season to 64. Once Air Force started to play it was each and every year with no years skipped. In this book we look at them all in chronological order. The coaches and certain games and certain players are highlighted within the seasons in which the games were played. I sure hope you enjoy this unique approach.

You will be impressed as you look at the highlights of the games and the coaches and players as to how many officers contributed to the many great Falcon football seasons. There's a lot of great reading in this book for sure.

With the current coach who has brought in great Air Force teams since taking the reins in 2007, would it not be wonderful for Air Force, the major defender of our Nation at in the AIR, to bring home a national football championship sometime soon

Your author would like you to know that when football season closes in the second week of January each year, there is now a great football item—this book—that is available all 52 weeks of the year and in fact all 365 days each year. It does not rely on the stadium gates being open for you to get a great dose of Air Force Football. Just begin reading right here.

It is now available for you to add to your Air Force Football experience. and your book collection. Once you get this book, it is yours forever unless, of course you give it away to one of the many who will be in awe, and who will accept it gladly. For those who love to use gadgets to read, this book is also available electronically on sources such as Kindle.

We open the season chronology in this book in 1955 when Air Force was so new to the game that it played just Freshman teams. It then moves on to the first varsity game in 1956 with a powerful 6-2-1 season following the opener. The book takes you all the way to Troy Calhoun's great record. It tells a story about all the football seasons and all the great coaches from the first coached game in 1955 to today.

You are going to love this book because it is the perfect read for anybody who loves Air Force's storied football program and wants to know more about the most revered athletes to have competed in one of the finest football programs of all time.

Few sports books are a must-read but Brian Kelly's Great Moments in Air Force Football will quickly appear at the top of Americas most enjoyable must-read books about sports. Enjoy!

Who is Brian W. Kelly?

Brian W. Kelly is one of the leading authors in America with this, his 190th published book. Brian is an outspoken and eloquent expert on a variety of topics and he has also written several hundred articles on topics of interest to Americans.

Most of his early works involved high technology. Later, Brian wrote a number of patriotic books and most recently he has been writing human interest books such as The Wine Diet and Thank you, IBM. His books are always well received.

Brian's books are highlighted at www.letsgopublish.com. Quantities from 20 to 1000 of any book can be made available from www.letsgopublish.com. You will see most of Brian's works by taking the following link www.amazon.com/author/brianwkelly. At this site, you can buy one book if you choose or a million, more or less.

The Best!

Sincerely,

Brian W. Kelly, Author
Brian P. Kelly, Editor in Chief
I am Brian Kelly's eldest son.

Table of Contents

Chapter 1 Introduction to Air Force Football 1

Chapter 2 The Founding of the United States Air Force Academy 9

Chapter 3 Air Force Fields & Stadiums 19

Chapter 4 First Two Coaches: Whitlow & Shaw 23

Chapter 5 Coach Ben Martin 1958-1967 31

Chapter 6 Coach Ben Martin 1968-1977 45

Chapter 7 Coach Bill Parcells 1978-1978 57

Chapter 8 Coach Ken Hatfield 1979-1983 63

Chapter 9 Coach Fisher DeBerry 1984-1995 75

Chapter 10 Coach Fisher DeBerry 1996-2006 99

Chapter 11 Coach Troy Calhoun 2007-2016 137

Chapter 12 Coach Troy Calhoun 2017-2018 173

Other Books by Brian Kelly: (amazon.com, and Kindle) 179

About the Author

Brian Kelly retired as an Assistant Professor in the Business Information Technology (BIT) Program at Marywood University, where he also served as the IBM i and Midrange Systems Technical Advisor to the IT Faculty. Kelly designed, developed, and taught many college and professional courses. He continues as a contributing technical editor to a number of technical industry magazines, including "The Four Hundred" and "Four Hundred Guru," published by IT Jungle.

Kelly is a former IBM Senior Systems Engineer. His specialty was problem solving for customers as well as implementing advanced operating systems and software on his client's machines. Brian was a certified Army Instructor before retiring. He is the author of 194 books and hundreds of magazine articles. He has been a frequent speaker at technical conferences throughout the United States.

Brian was a candidate for the US Congress from Pennsylvania in 2010 and he ran for Mayor in his home town in 2015. He loves Air Force Football and can't wait to see the Falcons have another great season in 2019 with another Commander-in-Chief's Trophy. God bless the Air Force Falcons!!!

Chapter 1 Introduction to Air Force Football

Air Force's 65th Year in 2019!

Falcons' head coach Troy Calhoun leads Air Force on to the field at Falcon Stadium, Sept. 3, 2016 to take on the Abilene Christian University Wildcats. Air Force beat Abilene 37-21.

The Air Force Falcons football team represents the United States Air Force Academy in college football. Air Force is currently a Division I Mountain West Conference member of the NCAA. The Falcons currently play their home games in Falcon Stadium, which is an outdoor football stadium in the western United States, located on the campus of the U.S. Air Force Academy in Colorado Springs, Colorado. It has a current seating capacity of 46,692.

Falcon Stadium of course is the home field of the Air Force Falcons of the Mountain West Conference. Air Force also holds the academy's graduation ceremonies there each spring.

Air Force is currently coached by Troy Calhoun, who is in his 13th season as head coach. Air Force has never won a national championship, but they have come as close as you can twice and were ranked in the AP poll six times. Considering that of the 130 NCAA Division I teams, they have the sixth youngest program, Air Force has a lot of years to get their championships.

Officially the Air Force recognize a relatively short but great football history that dates back to 1955 when they played their first game. If you are from Army or Navy, you have to be kind. Such rivals know that Air Force born great and the Academy gets greater as the program prospered under a number of fine coaches.

Coach: Troy Calhoun's record after 2017 was (82-60) in 11 seasons at Air Force. In 2018, the Falcons were 5-7 bringing Calhoun's record to 87-67. In 2017, they tied for 4th in Mountain Division and they lost to both Army and Navy. In 2018, they came back and whipped Navy but lost by three points to Army. We know how important the service games are.

In 2017 QB Arion Worthman threw for 1,115 yards and 10 TDs and ran for 831 yards and 13 TDs last season), WR Ronald Cleveland claimed 418 yards and 3 TDs rushing, 261 yards and 2 TDs receiving, , RB Nolan Eriksen (averaged 5.7 yards a carry on 40 attempts in 2018), LB Kyle Floyd (Falcons' No. 4 tackler last year with 60), S James Jones (No. 5 tackler with 52.

Despite a few great games, both 2017 and 2018 were disappointing for Air Force, but the Falcons never give up.

We begin the rest of the Air Force football story in Chapter 2 with the founding of US Air Force Academy in April 1954 in Colorado. and we continue in subsequent chapters, right into the founding of the full Air Force football program in 1955.

In defining the format of the book, we chose to use a timetable that is based on a historical chronology. Within this framework, we discuss the great moments in Air Force football history, and there are many great moments. No book can claim to be able to capture them all, as it would be a never-ending story, but we sure do try.

Chapter 1 Introduction to Air Force Football 3

Air Force Game Pageantry tops them all

Even if it is not an Air Force game

An A-10 Thunderbolt II does a show of force maneuver after locating a simulated downed pilot during Red Flag-Alaska 13-3, Aug. 22, 2013, at Eielson Air Force Base, Alaska. Two A-10s defended the pilot's position until members of the 210th Rescue Squadron could rescue him. The A-10 is assigned to the 163rd Fighter Squadron, Indiana Air National Guard, Fort Wayne, Ind. (U.S. Air Force photo/Senior Airman Shawn Nickel)

No matter how great an Army or Navy or Notre Dame pep rally may be, there is nothing that compares with the tools the US Air Force has in its arsenal. The mission of the Falcons is to defend the country by air. And, of course when the Air Force decides to strut its stuff, no school and in fact, no nation in the world can compare—even another US service academy.

An example was this year's (2018) Notre Dame game when four U.S. Air Force A-10 Thunderbolts will perform a flyover before Vanderbilt and Notre Dame kick off on Saturday. The Falcons actually can take credit when the flyover is not for a Falcons game.

The following "Blacksnakes" from the 163rd Fighter Squadron performed the flyover: Lt. Col. Brian "Mad Dawg" Frazier, Maj. Rod "JOBU" Metzler, Lt. Col. Kurt "Kid" Martin and Maj. Travis "Spades" Walton. It was great.

Split second timing is the only way. The flyover occurred at 2:28 p.m. as the Band of the Fighting Irish concluded the National Anthem. Fans were able to watch the flyover live on Countdown to Kickoff, which aired from 1:30-2:30 p.m. Try to beat a flyover.

HEAD COACH TROY CALHOUN

The purpose of the United States Air Force Academy is to develop young people of strong character who graduate and serve as outstanding leaders on active duty and beyond. It's a purpose Troy Calhoun thoroughly respects and realizes is necessary for our country. Calhoun left the Houston Texans of the NFL as an offensive coordinator in 2007 to embrace the mission of the Air Force Academy and accomplish what was once considered nearly impossible: building a service academy program that often earns a postseason bid while playing in one of college football's best conferences. Seven of his eight years Air Force has been to a bowl under Calhoun's guidance. The coach has guided Air Force to a 59-44 career record entering his ninth season.

Air Force student-athletes must complete the nation's most demanding academic curriculum while further embedding the heart and character that are crucial for serving America. Cadets at the Academy work through courses that require finishing over 140 semester hours. Strong character traits, to include respect, teamwork, courage, spirit, discipline, honesty and toughness, are the bedrock of the leadership qualities Air Force football players utilize while serving as officers in the United States Air Force. Calhoun and his staff have come up with a way to manage the varied demands of their players and lead them into a cohesive team that has fared quite well both on and off the field in his eight seasons as head coach.

Calhoun's players are extraordinarily successful finishing their academic and leadership responsibilities. The Air Force football team's NCAA APR (Academic Progress Report) is annually amongst the finest of the 127 schools that play at the FBS level of college football. From May 2007 through the present, Air Force Football's multi-year APR has finished above the nation's 90th percentile six of the last eight years which is more than any sport at any service academy. Air Force football's most recent Graduation Success Rate (GSR) is 93 percent. In addition to being one of the nation's best in regards to the NCAA's APR and GSR, 169 of 170 seniors (99%) who have played for Calhoun since 2007 have graduated from the United States Air Force Academy and served as officers for our nation.

Calhoun is the only coach in the history of service academy team ball sports to lead teams to a post-season bid six consecutive years. They have done this while playing very strong opponents. Calhoun's 2009 Air Force squad was the only team in the last 50 years of service academy football to play at least four ranked teams and win a bowl game in the same season. In the

100-plus year history of service academy football, Calhoun is the first coach to lead teams to at least six wins and a bowl game in each of his first six seasons.

Calhoun's 2014 team finished 10-3 overall while having all 28 seniors graduate from the Air Force Academy. Calhoun was named as a finalist for the Maxwell National Coach of the Year. The Falcons qualified for their seventh bowl game in eight years, and by winning the Famous Idaho Potato Bowl, captured their third bowl championship since 2009. Air Force defeated Army and Navy to win a record 19th Commander-in-Chief's Trophy and its third CINC title in the last five years. The Falcons were also one of just two teams nationally to beat two 10-win teams in the regular season. The Falcons beat Boise State and in-state rival Colorado State, who each won 10-plus games. Air Force's 10-win season was the first this century for the Academy and just

the ninth in the last 100 years of service academy football. The team finished 6-0 at home for just the third time in school history. Calhoun's 2007 squad also finished 6-0 at home.

Air Force earned a bid in 2012 to the Armed Forces Bowl. Air Force won its second straight Commander-in-Chief's Trophy (then-record 18th overall) in 2011, the first back-to-back titles at the Academy since 2001-02 and earned their fifth straight bowl game in the Military Bowl. The 2010 Air Force team finished 9-4 overall and won Air Force's 17th Commander-in-Chief's Trophy championship with wins over Army and Navy. The Falcons closed the 2010 season with a victory over Georgia Tech of the ACC in the Independence Bowl. Calhoun was named Coach of the Year by the Colorado Chapter of the National Football Foundation.

The 2009 Air Force team finished 8-5 overall and concluded with a convincing 47-20 win over 25th-ranked Houston in the Bell Helicopter Armed Forces Bowl. Air Force set 13 Academy bowl team records in the dominant victory. The team also set six school records during the 2009 season. Calhoun was named Coach of the Year by the Colorado Chapter of the National Football Foundation for his efforts.

Calhoun's 2007 and 2008 Air Force teams finished 9-4 and 8-5, respectively, and both earned bowl bids. The 2007 Falcons were the only team in Air Force history to win road games at Notre Dame, Utah and Colorado State in the same season. The five-game turnaround from 2006, in which Air Force was 4-8, was the largest in the nation that season by a first-year

Troy Calhoun enters his ninth season in 2015

Coach Calhoun's Note to Air Force Football Fans

To the great fans of the Air Force Falcons,

Welcome to the United States Air Force Academy - one of the world's finest educational and leadership institution. The purpose of the Academy is to develop young men and women of strong character to serve as outstanding leaders for our nation. The integrity, pride, and purpose of our future officers will make you quite proud.

Beginning with the entry of the first Academy class back in July of 1955, intercollegiate athletics continues to provide a crucial vehicle contributing to the profound leadership and valiancy Academy graduates carry forth to active duty and in their civilian lives. Air Force football has a three-pronged aim: on-field competitive spirit, instilling within our cadets lifelong resolute character traits, and preparing each team member for service and leadership to
help our country.

Your support, through purchases of season tickets, is crucial to the future sustainability of our cadet programs. Our commitment
to our friends, cadets and supporters is to provide the nation's best fan experience. It includes ease of parking, unmatched pageantry and the finest ticket value in all of college football.

In conclusion, if you find the qualities of honesty, passion, toughness and service appealing, then you will be proud to embrace and support the 2015 Air Force Football team.

Thank you in advance for your unwavering commitment to the Air Force Academy and our exciting Falcons.
Sincerely,

Troy Calhoun

Coach Troy Calhoun
Air Force Football

Chapter 2 The Founding of the United States Air Force Academy

US Air Force Academy Campus

Our deep thanks to the military for providing this great piece of history available publicly for your edification and enjoyment.

The United States Army was flying planes and providing tactical air service for a long time before the "Air Force" came into being.

Air Force News *Early Years*

On Aug. 1, 1907, the U.S. Army Signal Corps established a small Aeronautical Division to take "charge of all matters pertaining to military ballooning, air machines and all kindred subjects."
The Signal Corps began testing its first airplane at Fort Myer, Va., on Aug. 20, 1908, and on Sept. 9, Lt. Thomas E. Selfridge, flying with Orville Wright, was killed when the plane crashed. He was the first military aviation casualty. After more testing with an improved Wright

Flyer, the Army formally accepted this airplane, identified as "Airplane No. 1," on Aug. 2, 1909.

In early 1913, the Army ordered its aviators who were training in Augusta, Ga., and Palm Beach, Fla., to Texas to take part in 2d Division maneuvers. In Galveston on March 3, the Chief Signal Officer designated the assembled men and equipment the "1st Provisional Aero Squadron," with Capt. Charles DeF. Chandler as squadron commander.

The 1st Provisional Aero Squadron began flying activities a few days later. On Dec. 4, general orders re-designated the unit as the 1st Aero Squadron, effective Dec. 8, 1913. This first military unit of the U.S. Army devoted exclusively to aviation, today designated the 1st Reconnaissance Squadron, has remained continuously active since its creation. Assigned a role in the Punitive Expedition of the Mexican border in 1916, this squadron became the first air combat unit of the U.S. Army.

Meanwhile, Congress created in the Signal Corps an Aviation Section to replace the Aeronautical Division. Signed by the President, this bill became law on July 18, 1914. It directed the Aviation Section to operate and supervise "all military [U.S. Army] aircraft, including balloons and airplanes, all appliances pertaining to said craft, and signaling apparatus of any kind when installed on said craft."

The section would also train "officers and enlisted men in matters pertaining to military aviation," and thus embraced all facets of the Army's air organization and operation.

The old Aeronautical Division continued to exist but operated as the Washington office of the new section.

When World War I broke out in Europe in August 1914, the 1st Aero Squadron represented the entire tactical air strength of the U.S. Army. It counted 12 officers, 54 enlisted men and six aircraft. In December 1915 the Aviation Section consisted of 44 officers, 224 enlisted men and 23 airplanes--still a tiny force when compared to the fledgling air forces of the European powers.

But the war in Europe focused more attention on aviation.

By this time the Aviation Section consisted of the Aeronautical Division, the Signal Corps Aviation School at San Diego, the 1st Aero Squadron (then on duty with the expeditionary force in Mexico), and the 1st Company, 2d Aero Squadron, on duty in the Philippines. In October 1916, Aviation Section plans called for two dozen squadrons-- seven for the Regular Army, 12 for the National Guard divisions, and five for coastal defense -- plus balloon units for the field and coast artillery.

In December 1916 the seven Regular Army squadrons either had been or were being organized. All 24 squadrons had been formed by early 1917, but the 1st Aero Squadron remained the only one fully organized and equipped. Plans for still greater expansion of the Aviation Section were incomplete when the United States entered World War I on April 6, 1917.

World War I

On May 20, 1918, President Woodrow Wilson issued an executive order transferring aviation from the Signal Corps to two agencies under the Secretary of War: The Bureau of Aircraft Production, headed by Mr. John D. Ryan, and the Division of Military Aeronautics, directed by Maj. Gen. William L. Kenly.

On May 24 the War Department officially recognized these two Army agencies as the Air Service of the U.S. Army. Three months later, on Aug. 27, the President appointed Mr. Ryan Director of the Air Service and Second Assistant Secretary of War.

The dispersal of aero squadrons among various Army organizations during the war made it difficult to coordinate aerial activities, which led to the creation of higher echelon organizations. At the front, squadrons with similar functions were formed into groups, the first organized in April 1918 as I Corps Observation Group. The following month the 1st Pursuit Group was formed, and in July 1918 the American Expeditionary Forces organized its first aircraft unit higher than a group--the 1st Pursuit Wing--made up of the 2d and 3d Pursuit Groups and, later, the 1st Day Bombardment Group. In November 1918 the AEF possessed 14 groups (seven observation, five pursuit and two bombardment).

Following the armistice, demobilization of the Air Service was rapid and thorough.

At war's end the Air Service possessed 185 aero squadrons; 44 aero construction; 114 aero supply, 11 aero replacement, and 150 spruce production squadrons; 86 balloon companies; six balloon group headquarters; 15 construction companies; 55 photographic sections; and a few miscellaneous units.

By Nov. 22, 1919, all had been demobilized except one aero construction, one aero replacement, and 22 aero squadrons, 32 balloon companies, 15 photographic sections, and a few miscellaneous units. Between Nov.11, 1918 and June 30, 1920, officer strength plummeted from 19,189 to 1,168, and enlisted strength dropped from 178,149 to 8,428.

Following World War I, the strength of the Air Service matched what Congress considered satisfactory for peacetime.

Between Wars

The Army Reorganization Act of 1920 made the Air Service a combatant arm of the Army and gave the Chief of the Air Service the rank of major general and his assistant chief the rank of brigadier general. Tactical air units in the United States were placed under the nine U.S. Army corps area commanders where they continued to be employed primarily in support of the ground forces. The Chief of the Air Service retained command of various training schools, depots and other activities exempted from Army corps control.

During most of the 1920s, the total offensive strength of the Air Service in the United States consisted of one pursuit, one attack and one bombardment group. Overseas, the Canal Zone and the Philippines each had assigned one pursuit and one bombardment squadron with two squadrons of each type stationed in the Hawaiian Islands. The Air Service focused initially on observation and pursuit aviation, with major aeronautical development efforts concentrated in the Engineering Division at McCook Field, Dayton, Ohio.

The formal training establishment took shape during the 1920s. The Air Service concentrated flying training in Texas. Technical schools for officers and enlisted men were at Chanute Field, Ill. The Air Service (later, Air Corps) Tactical School trained officers to command higher units and taught the employment of military aviation. First located at Langley Field, Va., this school moved to Maxwell Field, Ala. in 1931.

The Air Corps Act of 1926 changed the name of the Air Service to Air Corps but left unaltered its status as a combatant arm of the U.S. Army.

The act also established the Office of Assistant Secretary of War for Air. The Air Corps had at this time 919 officers and 8,725 enlisted men, and its "modern aeronautical equipment" consisted of 60 pursuit planes and 169 observation planes; total serviceable aircraft of all types numbered less than 1,000.

In August 1926 the Army established the Air Corps Training Center in San Antonio, Texas. A few weeks later, on Oct. 15, the logistical organization was placed on firmer footing with the establishment of the Materiel Division, Air Corps, at Dayton, Ohio. A year later this division moved to nearby Wright Field, thereafter the primary base for air logistics.

On March 1, 1935, the General Headquarters Air Force, which had existed in gestation since Oct.1, 1933, became operational and assumed command and control over Air Corps tactical units. Tactical units, less some observation squadrons scattered throughout the nine Army corps areas, transferred to this initial air force.

The three GHQAF wings were located at Langley Field, Va.; Barksdale Field, La.; and March Field, Calif. The Office of the Chief of the Air Corps and GHQAF existed on the same command echelon, each reporting separately to the Army Chief of Staff. The GHQAF Commander directed tactical training and operations, while the Chief of the Air Corps maintained control over procurement, supply, training schools and doctrine development. On March 1, 1939, the Chief of the Air Corps assumed control over the GHQAF, centralizing command of the entire air arm.

President Franklin D. Roosevelt acknowledged the growing importance of airpower, recognized that the United States might be drawn into a European war. Assured of a favorable reception in the White House, the Air Corps prepared plans in October 1938 for a force of some 7,000 aircraft.

Soon afterwards, President Roosevelt asked the War Department to prepare a program for an Air Corps composed of 10,000 airplanes, of which 7,500 would be combat aircraft.

In a special message to Congress on January 12, 1939, the President formally requested this program. Congress responded on April 3, authorizing $300 million for an Air Corps "not to exceed 6,000 serviceable airplanes."

World War II

Beginning in September 1939, the German army and the German air force rapidly conquered Poland, Norway, Holland, Belgium, France and within one year had driven the British off the continent. Leaders of the Air Corps now found themselves in the novel position of receiving practically anything they requested. Plans soon called for 54 combat groups. This program was hardly underway before revised plans called for 84 combat groups equipped with 7,800 aircraft and manned by 400,000 troops by June 30, 1942. All told, U.S. Army air forces strength in World War II would swell from 26,500 men and 2,200 aircraft in 1939 to 2,253,000 men and women and 63,715 aircraft in 1945.

Both necessity and desire thus caused a blitz of organizational changes from 1940 through 1942. On November 19, 1940, the General Headquarters Air Force was removed from the jurisdiction of the Chief of the Air Corps and given separate status under the commander of the Army Field Forces. Seven months later, these air combat forces returned to the command of air leaders as Gen. George C. Marshall, U.S. Army Chief of Staff, established the Army Air Forces on June 20, 1941, to control both the Air Corps and the Air Force Combat Command.

Early in 1941, the War Department instituted a series of actions to create a hierarchy for noncombat activities. It set up a command eventually designated Flying Training Command to direct new programs for training ground crews and technicians. The next year, the new command assumed responsibility for pilot and aircrew training. In mid-1942 the War Department established the Air Corps Ferrying Command to fly aircraft overseas for delivery to the British and other Allies. As the functions of the Ferrying Command expanded, it was re-designated as the Air Transport Command.

The War Department reorganization on March 9, 1942, created three autonomous U.S. Army Commands: Army Ground Forces, Services of Supply (later, in 1943, Army Service Forces), and Army Air Forces. This administrative reorganization did not affect the status of the Air Corps as a combatant arm of the US Army.

Before 1939 the Army's air arm was a fledgling organization; by the end of the war the Army Air Forces had become a major military organization comprised of many air forces, commands, divisions, wings, groups, and squadrons, plus an assortment of other organizations.

Rapid demobilization of forces immediately after World War II, although sharply reducing the size of the Army Air Forces, left untouched the nucleus of the postwar United States Air Force (USAF). A War Department letter of March 21, 1946, created two new commands and re-designated an existing one: Continental Air

Forces was re-designated Strategic Air Command, and the resources of what had been Continental Air Forces were divided among Strategic Air Command and the two newcomers - Air Defense Command and Tactical Air Command.

These three commands and the older Air Transport Command represented respectively the strategic, tactical, defense, and airlift missions that provided the foundation for building the postwar, independent Air Force.

An Independent Force

The National Security Act of 1947 became law on July 26, 1947. It created the Department of the Air Force, headed by a Secretary of the Air Force.

Under the Department of the Air Force, the act established the United States Air Force, headed by the Chief of Staff, USAF. On Sept. 18, 1947, W. Stuart Symington became Secretary of the Air Force, and on Sept. 26, Gen. Carl A. Spaatz became the USAF's first Chief of Staff.

Army Air Corps

To recap, in the first major step toward an independent Air Force, the Army Air Service was re-designated, July 2, 1926, as advocates of air power fought for a separate branch under the Department of Defense, and others fought to keep the aviation assets within the Army command structure.

During this time, the primary mission of aviators was still to support troops on the ground and aviation assets still reported to ground forces commanders and not the Air Corps. The Air Corps staff was solely responsible for overseeing procurement, maintenance, supply and training.

The Air Corps also sought to grow the ranks of aviators and aircraft but never saw this to fruition because of a lack of funding during the Great Depression.

Although the Army Air Forces took the lead from the Army Air Corps in 1941, the Army Air Corps played a combat role in the Army and was not dissolved until 1947 - with the creation of the Air Force.

The Naval Academy Short Story: Courtesy of USAFA.af.mil

Taken from a work published January 18, 2012

The U.S Air Force Academy was established April 1, 1954, the culmination of an idea years in the making. Airpower leaders, long before the Air Force was a separate service, argued that they needed a school dedicated to war in the air, to train Airmen. After September 1947, when the Air Force was established as a separate service, this idea finally had the legitimacy of the new service behind it.

In 1948, seventy years ago, the Air Force appointed a board, later named the Stearns-Eisenhower Board for its chairmen, to study existing military academies and the options for an Air Force academy. Their conclusions were strongly put: The Air Force needed its own school; they additionally recommended at least 40 percent of future officers be service academy graduates.

After Congress passed a bill establishing the Air Force Academy, the secretary of the Air Force appointed a commission to recommend a location. After traveling 21,000 miles and considering hundreds of sites, the commission recommended Colorado Springs as its first choice. The secretary agreed, and the purchasing of the thousands of acres began. The state of Colorado contributed $1 million to the purchase of the land.

On July 11, 1955, the same year construction on the Academy began in Colorado Springs, the first class of 306 men was sworn-in at a temporary site, Lowry Air Force Base in Denver. Lieutenant Gen. Hubert R. Harmon, a key figure in the development of early plans for an Academy, was recalled from retirement by President Dwight D. Eisenhower to become the first Academy superintendent.

Two years later, Maj. Gen. James Briggs took over as the Academy's second superintendent. On Aug. 29, 1958, 1,145 cadets moved to the

Academy's permanent site from Denver. Less than a year later, the Academy received academic accreditation and graduated its first class of 207 June 3, 1959. In 1964, the authorized strength of the Cadet Wing increased to 4,417. The present authorized strength is approximately 4,000.

Perhaps the most controversial event in the Academy's history was the admission of women. President Gerald R. Ford signed legislation Oct. 7, 1975, permitting women to enter the military academies. Women first entered the Air Force Academy June 28, 1976. The first-class including women graduated in 1980 and included the Academy's first woman to be superintendent, retired Lt. Gen. Michelle Johnson.

The Academy celebrated the 50th anniversary of its inception April 1, 2004. Three noteworthy events occurred in connection with the celebration: a 37-cent commemorative stamp was issued honoring the Academy with the Cadet Chapel strikingly portrayed; the Academy was declared a national historic landmark with a plaque installed on the Honor Court to mark the occasion; and Harmon was officially named as the "Father of the Air Force Academy," honoring the pivotal role he played in its planning and establishment. Further anniversaries were marked during the next four years, culminating with the 50th anniversary of the first commencement at the Academy in 2009.

The Academy provides the Air Force with a corps of officers dedicated to upholding the high standards of their profession. The Air Force in turn provides a proving ground for these officers and sent back to its Academy dedicated staff members to educate and train future leaders. Fifty years after the first class entered, the Academy has graduated more than 50,000 officers intent on serving their country.

Chapter 3 Air Force Fields & Stadiums

Denver University's Hilltop Stadium

The Air Force Academy had no stadium in 1955 when it commenced its football program. So, until Falcon Stadium was built on the Air Force Academy Campus, football games and other sports were played not too far away in Denver University Stadium (DU) shown above.

Denver University Stadium was a stadium in the western United States, on the campus of the University of Denver in Denver, Colorado. It was once known as Hilltop Stadium. Built in 1926, the crescent-shaped main grandstand design on the west sideline was based on other similar-sized stadiums from the same the time period, Brown Stadium and Cornell's Schoellkopf Field, both in the Ivy League. There were few original designs in the early years.

The Stadium hosted the DU Pioneers college football team until the program was discontinued in 1961, due to mounting deficits. The stadium had a seating capacity of 30,000 at its peak, and the natural grass field had a conventional north-south orientation at an elevation of 5,350 feet (1,630 m) above sea level. Nearly a half century in age, it was torn down in the early 1970s. By this time, The Air Force Falcons had their own stadium on campus.

As noted, The U.S. Air Force Academy Falcons shared the stadium with DU until their Falcon Stadium opened in Colorado Springs in 1962. DU Stadium has some history of its own that you may find of interest. The professional Denver Broncos, then in the AFL, played 11 pre-season and 2 early regular season games at the DU stadium in the early and mid-1960s—after DU dropped football. The Broncos' home venue, Bears Stadium (later renamed "Mile High"), was shared with the Triple-A Denver Bears baseball club. For Air Force, it was an eternity but just seven years after its program began, the Falcons had their own modern (for the day) football stadium.

Falcon Stadium

In recent times, newcomers to Falcon Stadium will see it as one of the premier college football stadiums in America. Falcon football veterans, on the other hand, may not even recognize their old stomping grounds Prior to the 2006 season, FieldTurf was installed at a cost of $750,000. The new turf covers 84,480 square feet with an additional 26,520 square feet of native grass surrounding it.

There are approximately 380 tons of rubber and sand infill between the synthetic fibers. The surface is capable of draining up to 12 feet of water per hour thanks to the existing 1.5 miles of underground drainage pipe and 27 miles of heating cables.
In 2004, a new scoreboard was installed. The board features a huge video screen and message board and replaced the old board at the south end of the field. In 2002, the Academy added permanent lights.

The cost of just under $500,000 was at no expense to tax payers. The Air Force Academy Athletic Association picked up the tab.
In 1991, the Academy installed nine skyboxes and remodeled the existing press box. The facility now seats 450 people indoors, along with 88 in the skyboxes. In addition to its game-day uses, the press box is also used by the athletic department as a banquet/meeting room. Falcon Stadium was built in the fall of 1962 at a cost of $3.5 million.

The stadium, which was built in a natural bowl, has a capacity of 46,692 and stands in the base of the Rampart Range of the Rocky Mountains.

Falcon Stadium opened on Sept. 22, 1962, when a then-overflow crowd of 41,350 saw Air Force defeat Colorado State, 24-0. AFA held a formal dedication on Oct. 20, 1962, when Air Force hosted Oregon. The Ducks won the game, 35-20.

The stadium was originally built solely for football, but lacrosse plays all of its home matches in the stadium and several non-athletic events, such as the Academy's annual graduation, are also conducted there.

Chapter 4 First Two Coaches: Whitlow & Shaw

Coach #1   Robert V. Whitlow
Coach #2   Buck Shaw

Year	Coach	Record	Conf	Record
1955	Robert V. Whitlow	4-4-0	Indep	
1956	Buck Shaw	6–2–1	Ind	
1957	Buck Shaw	3–6–1	Ind	

Coach Robert Whitlow

(*Whitlow in his P-51 which bears markings from his two aerial kills on November 26, 1944*)

Colonel Robert V. Whitlow (November 7, 1918 – July 11, 1997) was the Air Force Academy's first football coach and their first athletic director. He was first an American military officer, and then a football coach, university athletic director, and sports club executive.

He served as the first head football coach and athletic director of the United States Air Force Academy in 1955. Whitlow had a twenty-year career in the United States Air Force, and during World War II, saw combat as both a bomber and fighter pilot. After his military service, he worked for the Chicago Cubs baseball franchise as its first "athletic director."

Robert Whitlaw, Eugene Vosika, Gregory Boyington, Jr., and Lawrence T. 'Buck' Shaw (Original Caption) Here comes the Air Force! Denver, Colorado: Since the Air Force has taken its place alongside the Army and Navy by having its own academy, it's only fitting that it should have a football team. The squad is located at its temporary home at Lowry Air Force base. These men for part of the power of the new team. Left to right are: Colonel Robert Whitlow, head football coach; Eugene Vosika, tackle of Bellevue, Nebraska and son of a Master Sergeant in the Strategic Air Command; Gregory Boyington, Jr., tackle of Burbank, California and the son of the World War II ace and Congressional Medal of Honor winner; and Lawrence T. 'Buck' Shaw, former coach of the San Francisco 49ers.

The Air Force Falcons football team represented the United States Air Force Academy in the 1955 college football season. It was their first season of intercollegiate football.

The Falcons did not have an official stadium during the season, and remained without one until the 1962 season when Falcon Stadium opened. They were led by first year head coach Robert V. Whitlow and played the first season for the Air Force Falcons football program.

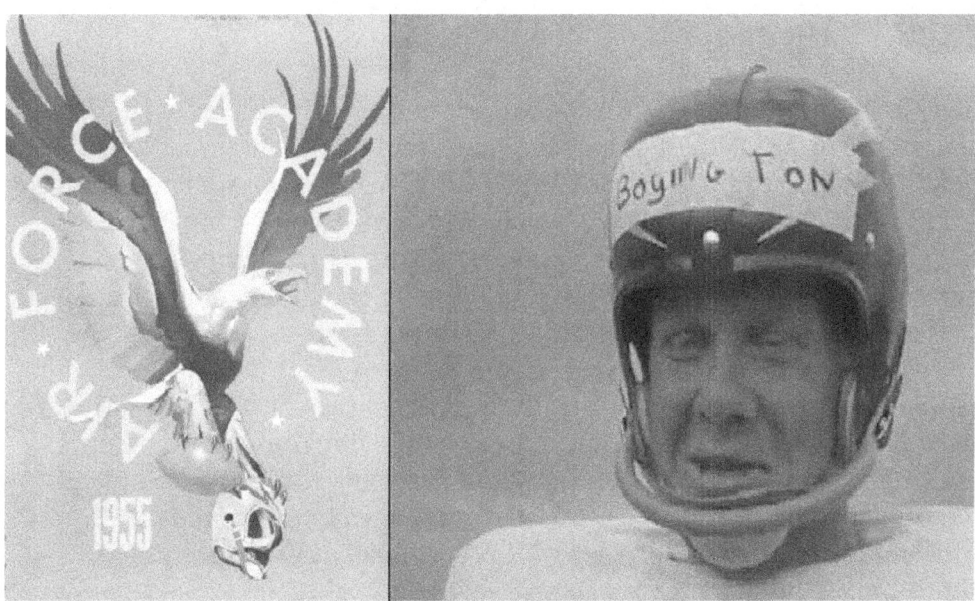

The Falcons were independent and played only freshmen teams of other schools. Air Force finished with a record of 4–4. The Falcons a number of teams from the Southwest this year including Denver, Colorado State, Colorado, Kansas, Utah, Wyoming, New Mexico and Oklahoma's freshmen teams and finished with a record of 4–4 as an independent.

The 1955 Football Season

All games but the November 19 encounter against the New Mexico Freshmen were played at the Denver U Field in Denver Colorado.

On Oct 8 against the Denver Freshmen, The Air Force Academy Falcons played their first game ever and grabbed their first victory when they defeated the Denver University Pioneers (Freshmen) W (34–18). They followed this with their second win in a row on Oct 15 against the Colorado State Freshmen W (W 21–13). Their first loss came by a shutout score of L (0-32) on Oct 22 when they were defeated by the Colorado Freshmen.

Then on Oct 29, the Falcons fell for the second time. Their opponent was the Kansas Freshmen and the result was a shutout loss L (0-33). That would be the lost shut out in 1955.

On Nov 5, the Utah Freshmen had just enough zip to barely beat the Falcons L (6-12). The Falcons began to win again on Nov 12, as they beat the Wyoming Freshmen W (21-13). The next outing was a nail-biter in which the Falcons prevailed on Nov 19 against the New Mexico Freshmen in a game played at Zimmerman Field, Albuquerque, NM   W (7–6). The Falcons ended the year with a loss on Nov 26 against the Oklahoma Freshmen L (48–12).

Considering that many colleges in their first years of play were forced to play football clubs, Junior Colleges, and even High School teams, playing Freshmen teams of a fledgling program was not a bad idea. The Falcons did quite well, considering that many were playing football for the first time. Their 4-4 record was quite respectable for these officer cadets.

Buck Shaw with his Air Force Academy Squad

Who is Coach Buck Shaw?

Buck Shaw was born on a farm in Michelville, Iowa, on March 28, 1899. With exactly four games of high school football behind him, he matriculated at Notre Dame, where he starred as a 6-foot, 175-pound tackle for Knute Rockne.

At the time he came to the Air Force, the 56-year-old Shaw had been a star player under Head Coach Knute Rockne at Notre Dame (where he was a teammate of the legendary George Gipp) and, with Rockne's encouragement, went on to coach at Santa Clara, Nevada, and North Carolina State before moving into the pro ranks as the original head coach of the San Francisco 49ers in the AAFC in 1946.

"The Silver Fox", as he was dubbed due to his full head of gray hair, stayed at the helm for nine years and his record with the 49ers, who became part of the NFL in 1950, was a solid 71-39-4. From there, he became the first head coach at the Air Force Academy, and resigned after going 9-8-2 in two seasons, he resigned his position. From the Academy, he joined the Philadelphia Eagles.

To help you know what kind of coach Shaw was, he was perfect for Air Force. In fact, he was perfect anywhere. After three years with the Eagles, he made it clear prior to the 1960 season that it would be his last. He went out on top. In making his retirement official the day after the Eagles won the championship, he said "I can't think of a better time to bow out. I can't soar any higher than being head coach of a world championship professional football team. It was a distinct pleasure coaching the Eagles, and I can't pay too high a tribute to this 1960 team. It was a team of tremendous desire, a team that just would not accept defeat."

Shaw returned to California and retirement with a 90-55-5 overall record as a pro head coach (AAFC and NFL) and 2-1 in the postseason. He was remembered long afterward as a quiet but firm gentleman who demanded top performance and molded a championship team, .

1956 Air Force Falcons Coach Buck Shaw

The Air Force Falcons football team represented the United States Air Force Academy in the 1956 college football season. It was their second season of intercollegiate football.

The Falcons still did not have an official stadium during the season, and remained without one until the 1962 season when Falcon Stadium opened. They were led by first year head coach Buck Shaw and played the second season for the Air Force Falcons football program.

The Falcons were independent, and unlike their first year, they played varsity teams of other schools. Air Force finished with a great record of 6-2-1. The Falcons played a number of teams from the Southwest this year much like the prior year.

Falcons home games were played at Denver University DU.

Games of the 1956 season

On Sep 29 at San Diego, The Air Force was victorious in a blowout W (46–0). On Oct 6 at Colorado College's Washburn Field in Colorado Springs, CO, the Air Force prevailed in another blowout. The Falcons were off to a great start. On Oct 13 at home, the Falcons ripped apart Western State W (48–13) for three in a row. The Falcons picked up their fourth win in a row on Oct 20 against the Colorado School of Mines in another blowout W (49–6)

It was five in a row after the Oct 27 encounter at home with Eastern New Mexico W (34–7). The Falcons appeared to be unbeatable and on Nov 3, they extended their win streak to 6-0 against Northern Colorado at home in a shutout at DU Stadium W (21–0). The first blemish on the Falcons record came on a tie played Nov 10 at Whittier College in CA T (14–14).

The first loss was on Nov 17 when Idaho State beat the Falcons by one TD in Pueblo, CO L (7–13). In another losing effort, BYU beat the Falcons at home L (7-13) ending a great season for Buck Shaw's Air Force Falcons.

1957 Air Force Falcons Coach Buck Shaw

The Air Force Falcons football team represented the United States Air Force Academy in the 1957 college football season. It was their second season of intercollegiate football.

The Falcons still did not have an official stadium during the season, and remained without one until the 1962 season when Falcon Stadium opened. They were led by second-year head coach Buck Shaw and played the third season for the Air Force Falcons football program with a record of 3-6-1.

The Falcons were independent. After a great year in 1956, Shaw's team slowed down a bit in 1957 only to erupt with wins galore in 1958. Falcons home games were played at Denver University DU.

The Air Force Academy itself spent its first three years housed at Lowry Air Force Base, Colorado, adjacent to Denver, until August 1958. Air Force did not play Army or Navy this particular season; Army was first played in 1959 and Navy in 1960.

Games of 1957 Season

Falcons home games were played at Denver University DU.

On Sep 20, at UCLA in the L.A. Memorial Coliseum in Los Angeles, CA, the Bruins defeated the Falcons in a shellacking L (0–47) before 33,293. On Sep 28, at home AFA whipped Occidental W 40–6. Then, on Oct 5, at home. The Falcons beat Detroit W (19–12).

At George Washington's Griffith Stadium on Oct 11 in Washington, D.C., The Falcons were defeated in a shutout L (0–20) before 12,000 On Oct 26 at Tulsa in Skelly Stadium, Tulsa, OK, the Golden Hurricane beat UFA L (7–12). At Wyoming on Nov 2 in the War Memorial Stadium, Laramie, WY, the Cowboys tied the Falcons T (7–7).

Then, on Nov 9 at Denver in DU Stadium , Denver, CO, the Pioneers beat the Falcons L (14–26). At Utah, on Nov 16 Ute Stadium, Salt Lake City, UT the Utes shut out the Falcons L (0–34). Then, on November 23 at home, the Air Force beat New Mexico W (34–21). At home on Nov. Colorado State beat AFA in a rivalry match L (7–20).

Chapter 5 Coach Ben Martin 1958-1967

Martin   Coach #3

Year	Coach	Record	Conference Record
1958	Ben Martin	9–0–2	Indep
1959	Ben Martin	5–4–1	Indep
1960	Ben Martin	4–6	Indep
1961	Ben Martin	3–7	Indep
1962	Ben Martin	5–5	Indep
1963	Ben Martin	7–4	Indep
1964	Ben Martin	4–5–1	Indep
1965	Ben Martin	3–6–1	Indep
1966	Ben Martin	4–6	Indep
1967	Ben Martin	2–6–2	Indep

NOVEMBER 8: Air Force Head Coach Ben Martin stands on the sidelines during an NCAA game against the Denver Pioneers on November 8, 1958 at DU Stadium in Denver, Colorado

Coach Ben Martin took the job of Head Coach for the Air Force very seriously and he spent a very productive 20 years with the Falcons. In this Chapter, we highlight his first ten seasons and in the next chapter, we cover his last ten.

Ben Martin, the former Air Force coach known widely as the Father of Air Force Football, was one heck of a football coach. He passed away on July 31, 2004 at the Village at Skyline in Colorado Springs. He was 83 years old.

<<< Coach Martin

There is always a prime mover in the beginning of a new football program. Martin came along in year four of the program after two head coaches and a lot of administrators had gotten the Air Force program rolling. He was the coach that helped America see the Air Force program as not only viable but phenomenally competitive.

Like most early outings of new football teams, the Falcons were just breaking in their flight jackets when Martin arrived. Nobody denies that it was Ben Martin who put Air Force football on the map during his 20-year (1958-77) coaching tenure. His first season set the stage for nineteen more as he hit the ground running, or he hit the skies passing, no matter which way you put it with a spectacular 9-02 first-year coaching record. Whew!

His short, controlled passing game enabled the much-smaller but always tough Falcons to compete on a national scale. Martin engineered upset victories over national powers Nebraska in 1963, UCLA in 1964, Washington in 1966, North Carolina in 1969, Stanford in 1970 and Arizona State in 1972.

The coach led the Falcons to three bowl games, including the 1959 Cotton Bowl, 1963 Gator Bowl and 1971 Sugar Bowl. The Cotton and Sugar bowl games mark the only New Year's Day bowl games Air Force has participated in.

Martin's undefeated 1958 team, his first at Air Force, is still considered one of the top teams in college football history. The Falcons went 9-0-1 in the regular season before battling to a 0-0 tie with Texas Christian in the Cotton Bowl to finish 9-0-2. The undefeated team is still the only one in Academy history.

That team featured the school's first consensus All-American, tackle Brock Strom. He and starting quarterback Rich Mayo went on to be inducted into the Verizon Academic All-American Hall of Fame in the 1990s. Wide receiver Ernie Jennings, a star on the 1970 team, also went on to earn consensus All-American honors and finished eighth in the Heisman Trophy balloting that year.

Martin's 20-year stint is the second-longest in-service academy football history and his 96-103-9 record at Air Force is the second-best in school history. Only long-time Falcon mentor Fisher DeBerry's 21-year tenure and 156-88-1 career record are better in each category.

At the time of his passing, there were many tributes that were provided as testimony to this fine coach. "This is a sad time for Falcon football," DeBerry said. "We enjoy a national prominence because of the foundation Ben Martin built. He will always be the Father of Falcon football. He was a great inspiration to me and a great mentor. He will be greatly missed in our community. He is one of the greatest coaches ever and was such a great commentator."

Martin was a 1946 graduate of the Naval Academy where he was a three-year letter winner in football and track (1942-44). In 1944, he earned the Thompson Trophy Cup, which is presented to the Midshipman to have done the most during the year for the promotion of athletics at the Naval Academy.

After a stint of sea duty in the Navy, Martin returned to the Naval Academy as an assistant coach from 1949-54. Navy's 1954 "Team Named Desire" squad went 8-2 and defeated Mississippi, 21-0, in the Sugar Bowl. Martin left Navy following that season to become the head coach at Virginia. He coached the Cavaliers for two seasons before taking over at Air Force.

Martin authored two books on football while coaching, "Ben Martin's Flexible-T Offense" and "End Play." He also coached in several all-star games, including the East-West Shrine game and the North-South game. Following his retirement in 1977, Martin went to work for ABC Sports as a color analyst. He returned to the Academy in 1987 and spent 16 seasons as Air Force's color analyst for radio broadcast before retiring following the 2002 season.

A native of Prospect Park, Pa., Martin attended Hill Preparatory School and Princeton University before his appointment to the Naval Academy.

1958 Air Force Falcons Coach Ben Martin

In 1958, the Air Force Academy made their first AP and coaches poll appearances, as well as their first bowl appearance in the Cotton Bowl against TCU, which ended in a scoreless tie. For want of a safety or a positive score of any kind, it is possible that Air Force would have been National Champions in 1958 in just their fourth year of operation. Air Force did not play Army or Navy this season; Army was first played in 1959 and Navy in 1960.

Games of the 1958 Season

Falcons home games were played at Denver University DU.

On Sep 26 at Detroit at the University of Detroit Stadium in Detroit, Michigan, the indefatigable Falcons plowed through to a great blowout win W (37–6).

Then, on Oct 4 at #8 ranked Iowa in Iowa Stadium, Iowa City, Iowa, the Hawkeyes and the Falcons played to an exiting tie finish T (13–13). Until the Cotton Bowl, that would be the only blemish on this undefeated team's record.

On Oct 11, at home, rivalry Colorado State was felled and overpowered by the invincible Air Force Falcons W (36–6). Against National powerhouse Stanford on Oct 18 at Stanford Stadium in Stanford, California, in a battle of the national birds, the Falcons defeated the Cardinal W (16–0). In another tough game played against a fine college football team, on Oct 25, # 14 Air Force squeaked by a tough Utah team at home W (16–14). Moving up in the rankings at # 13 now, on Nov 1, the Falcons emerged victorious in another close battel against Oklahoma State at Lewis Field in Stillwater, Oklahoma W (33–29).

At home again and sporting a #10 national ranking looking for an easy game, on Nov 8, the Falcons did not find one at Denver, but they stood tough and beat the Pioneers, who shared their stadium by a close score of W (10–7). Again ranked #10, on Nov 15, The Falcons beat Wyoming in a game played at Colorado Springs, Colorado W (21–6). Finally an easy game came along and the #9 Falcons were ready on Nov 22, at New Mexico as they whopped their opponent at Zimmerman Field in Albuquerque, New Mexico W (45–7) Now ranked at #8 nationally, on Nov 29, the Falcons played a tough game v Colorado and prevailed at Folsom Field in Boulder, Colorado W (20–14).

Cotton Bowl Classic

The Falcons finished the season undefeated at 9-0-1 and were invited to the **Cotton Bowl.**

#8 Air Force played a great game on January 1, 1959 vs. TCU in the Cotton Bowl Stadium in Dallas, Texas in a bowl game known as (Cotton Bowl Classic). The game was so tough neither team, who had a number of high scoring game wins in their season could score a point and thus tied each other on CBS TV and the rest of the nation by a score of zip-zip, T (0–0) before 75,504

The 1959 Cotton Bowl Classic featured the TCU Horned Frogs and the Air Force Falcons. The game was played on January 1, 1959, at the Cotton Bowl in Dallas, Texas. There had never been a tie in the game. In eleven years of play, this was the first tie in the game. Worse than that for fan enjoyment, it was a scoreless tie.

It was our undefeated Air Force that had already played to a tie during the 1958 regular season, 13–13 to Iowa who competed in this game. The Iowa Hawkeyes went on to win the Big Ten Conference and the Rose Bowl. The Falcons were ranked in the polls for the seventh straight week, #8 for the second straight week. They made their first-ever bowl appearance. They always played tough but sometimes tough is not enough.

Although it had snowed two days earlier, the field was clear, and the weather was sunny and 44 °F (7 °C) for the 2:30 p.m. CST kickoff.[3][4]

Game summary

In the end, it was six lost fumbles (out of 13 in total) and five missed field goals that decided the scoreless outcome. The Falcons at one point had the ball at TCU's 6-yard line before being stuffed, but when they tried to kick a field goal from the 12, George Pupich's kick sailed wide left. Pupich missed two more --one from 34 and the other from 52—while TCU missed two of their own.

TCU went 3 for 11 on passing for a woeful 37 yards but had 190 yards rushing on 48 attempts. Air Force barely did better with 12 for 23 passing for 91 yards and two interceptions. Both teams finished with over 227 yards yet had more punts (16) then points. Dave Phillips of Air Force and Jack Spikes of TCU were named Outstanding Players. One thing for sure, this Cotton Bowl game was a real battle which nobody wanted to lose.

1959 Air Force Falcons Coach Ben Martin

Games of the season

At Wyoming on Sep 26 in the War Memorial Stadium • Laramie, WY, the Falcons prevailed W (20–7). Then, on Oct 3 at Trinity in Alamo Stadium, San Antonio, TX, AFA won the game W (27–6). On Oct 10 at home, #18 AFA defeated Idaho in a shutout W (21–0) before 17,393. Oregon was next on Oct 17, as the #17 Falcons lost their first game of the season at Multnomah Stadium, Portland, OR L (3–20) before 29,162. Then, on Oct 23 at UCLA in the Los Angeles Memorial Coliseum in LA, CA, the Falcons won W (20–7).

In the first Army-Air Force Game, on Oct 31 vs. Army in Yankee Stadium, Bronx, NY, the teams played to a scoring tie T (13–13) before 67,000. At Missouri on Nov 7, the #18 ranked Falcons were beaten at Memorial Stadium, Columbia, MO L (0–13) before 32,000. Then, on Nov 14 at Arizona in Folsom Field • Boulder, CO, the Falcons beat the Wildcats W (22–15) before 8,500.

On Nov 21, at home, New Mexico barely beat the Air Force in a well-fought match, L (27–28). Then on Nov 28 at Colorado in Folsom Field, Boulder, CO, the Falcons lost L (7–15) before 40,000

About the Commander-In-Chief's Trophy

Since Air Force would now and forever be involved in the Navy football schedule, it is the right time to acknowledge the existence of the Commander in Chief's Trophy. We pause below to explain it.

The Commander-in-Chief's Trophy is awarded to each season's winner of the American college football triangular series among the teams of the U.S. Military Academy (Army Black Knights), the U.S. Naval Academy (Navy Midshipmen), and U.S. Air Force Academy (Air Force Falcons).

The Navy–Air Force game is traditionally played on the first Saturday in October, the Army–Air Force game on the first Saturday in November, and the Army–Navy Game on the second Saturday in December. In the event of a tie, the award is shared, but the previous winner retains possession of the trophy. Along with the Florida Cup, the Michigan MAC Trophy, and the Beehive Boot, the Commander-in-Chief's Trophy is one of the few three-way rivalries that awards a trophy to the winner.

Through 2017, the Air Force Falcons hold the most trophy victories at 20 and the Navy Midshipmen have won 15. The Army Black Knights trail with only seven; their last came just a year ago in 2017. The trophy has been shared on four occasions, last in 1993.

The first Navy v Air Force game came in 1960.

1960 Air Force Falcons Coach Ben Martin

Air Force was outscored by their opponents 147–178 and finished with a record of 4 wins and 6 losses (4–6).

This was the first year the Falcons played Navy. They endured a 35–3 loss in mid-October in this first Navy encounter at Memorial Stadium in Baltimore. Heisman Trophy winner Joe Bellino was at his best, scoring three first half touchdowns. Bellino also had an interception. The two academies met in even-numbered years (except 1962 and 1964) through 1971 and have played annually in the competition (with Army) for the Commander-in-Chief's Trophy, first awarded in 1972.

Games of the season

In the home opener at DU Stadium in Denver Colorado, the Air Force Falcons on Sep 24 overwhelmed Colorado State W (32–8). Against national contender Stanford on Oct 1, at home, the Falcons beat the Cardinal W 32–9. On Oct 8, at home, #11 Missouri defeated Air Force L (8–34). In the first match in what was to become a long series, # 5 ranked Navy overwhelmed the Air Force on Oct 15 at Memorial Stadium in Baltimore, MD L (3–35).

On Oct 22 at Wyoming's War Memorial Stadium in Laramie, WY, the Cowboys shut out the Falcons L (0–15). On Oct 29 at home, George Washington beat the Air Force L (6–20). On Nov 5 at home, the Falcons defeated Denver, W 36–6. On Nov 12 at #11 UCLA in Los Angeles Memorial Coliseum, Los Angeles, CA , the Bruins beat the Falcons L (0–22).

Then, on Nov 19 at Colorado in Folsom Field, Boulder, CO, the Falcons beat the Buffaloes W (16–6). In the season finale, on Dec 2 in the warmth of Miami, FL, in Orange Bowl Stadium, the Hurricanes beat the Falcons on Dec 2 L (14–23)
#Rankings from AP Poll.

1961 Air Force Falcons Coach Ben Martin

Both Army and Navy were off Air Force's schedule this season and the next, when the new Falcon Stadium opened.

Games of the Season

In the home opener on Sep 23 v UCLA in DU Stadium, Denver, CO, the Bruins defeated the Falcons L (6–19). Again at home, Kansas State edged out the Air Force on Sep 30 L (12–14). Then, on Oct 7 at SMU, the Mustangs nosed out the Falcons in Cotton Bowl Stadium, Dallas, TX L (7–9). At Cincinnati's Nippert Stadium in Cincinnati, OH on Nov 14, the Falcons prevailed over the Bearcats W (8–6). Then, on Oct 21, at home, Maryland shut out Air Force L (0–21) before 21,500.

On Oct 28 at New Mexico's University Stadium in Albuquerque, NM, the Lobos got the best of the Falcons L (6–21). On Nov 4 at home, Air Force defeated Colorado State in a close match W (14–9). At California's Memorial Stadium in Berkeley, CA , on Nov 11, the Falcons beat the Golden Bears W (15–14) before 38,000. At Baylor on Nov 18 in Baylor Stadium , WAC, TX, the Bears beat the Falcons L (7–31). Wrapping it up for 1961, #7 Colorado beat Air Force on Dec 2 in Folsom Field, Boulder, CO L (12–29) before 23,287

1962 Air Force Falcons Coach Ben Martin

On September 21, 1962, in the, season, home, and stadium opener for the 1962 Air Force Falcons, Air Force took the opportunity to soundly shut out Colorado State in the brand-new Falcon Stadium grand opening in Colorado Springs, CO W (34–0). Moving to the northeast against a powerful #4 ranked Penn State team, the Nittany Lions defeated the Air Force Falcons on Sep 28 in Beaver Stadium, University Park, PA L (6–20). On Oct 5 at SMU in the Cotton Bowl, Dallas, TX, the Falcons defeated the Mustangs W (25–20). On Oct 12 at Arizona in Arizona Stadium, Tucson, AZ, the Falcons beat the Wildcats W (20–6).

Then, on Oct 19 at home, Oregon beat Air Force L (20–35). On Oct 26 at home, the Miami Hurricanes defeated the Air Force Falcons L (3-21). On Nov 3, Air Force defeated Wyoming W (35–14). At UCLA on Nov 10 in Los Angeles Memorial Coliseum, Los Angeles, the Falcons got the best of the Bruins W (17–11). On Nov 17 at home, Baylor beat the Air Force L (3–10). Wrapping up what to that point was ae winning season, Colorado brought the Air Force Record to a 50-50 draw (5-5) with this defeat of the Falcons on Nov 24 at Colorado's Folsom Field in Boulder, CO   L (10–34).

1963 Air Force Falcons Coach Ben Martin

On September 21, 1962, in the, season and home opener for the 1963 Air Force Falcons, Air Force took the opportunity to defeat #10 Washington in the one-year old Falcon Stadium in Colorado Springs, CO W (10-7). On Sept 28, at home, the Falcons showed Colorado State what a fiery offense is all about as the team went into afterburner mode to wallop the Rams W (69-0). Then, at SMU on Oct 5, in the Cotton Bowl, Dallas, TX, the Mustangs defeated the Falcons L (0–10). At Nebraska on Oct 12 at Memorial Stadium in Lincoln, NE, the Falcons beat the Cornhuskers W (17–13). At Maryland on Oct 19 in Byrd Stadium , College Park, MD, the Terrapins beat the Falcons L (14–21).

On Oct 25, at home, in their first meeting, Air Force defeated Boston College W 34–7. After a short hiatus, with the stadium now completed, the series with Army was on again, On Nov 2 at Soldier Field in Chicago, Il, the Army beat the Air Force in a close match, L (10–14). On Nov9, at home, Air Force pounded UCLA W (48-0) . Then, at New Mexico on Nov 16, in University Stadium, Albuquerque, NM, the Falcons beat the Lobos W (30–8). In the final game of 1963 at home, Air Force defeated Colorado on Dec 7 W (17–14).

With seven wins, the Air Force qualified for a bowl game and were selected to play on December 28, 1963 vs. North Carolina in the Gator Bowl at Gator Bowl Stadium in Jacksonville, FL (Gator Bowl). The Tar Heels dominated play and beat the Falcons L (0–35).

1963 Gator Bowl Highlights

It had been four years since the Air Force last played in a Bowl Game. The Tar Heels were co-champions of the Atlantic Coast Conference, which was their first conference title since the 1949 Southern Conference Title. It was NC's Conference title and their first bowl game 1950.

There was no scoring by the Air Force in this game so the play-by play for scores is quite simple. The scoring included Willard's 1-yard and the kick was missed. Edge got a 6 yd TD run and this time the non-kick extra point did not work. Robinson scored on a 5-yard pass from Black. Kessler made it in on a 1-yard run and finally Black scored on a 5-yard run and Chapman got the kick through this time. Willard was the game hero for NC with 94 yards on 18 carries.

It was a long time for either team to have luck in a bowl game. Air Force's next shot was in 1971, but the Falcons did not win a bowl game until 1982. North Carolina took its time also and were not back in a bowl game until 1970. The game was marred by rumors of a game party at the Hotel Roosevelt in downtown Jacksonville. 22 died in the fire. The game got the blame, but it was a false claim as an investigation proved that the participants had nothing to do with the game. It was an unfortunate situation but for years, the blame stayed with the game, though untrue.

1964 Air Force Falcons Coach Ben Martin

This was the third year for the Falcons in their almost new Falcon Stadium in Colorado Springs, Colorado. They were outscored by their opponents 106–146 and finished with a record of 4 wins, 5 losses, and 1 tie (4–5–1).

On Sep 19 at #7 Washington, in the season opener the Falcons beat the Huskies in Husky Stadium, Seattle, WA, W (3–2). On Sep 26 at Michigan's Michigan Stadium in Ann Arbor, MI, the Wolverines beat the Falcons L (7–24). On Oct 3 at home, the Falcons beat Colorado State W (14-6). Then, in their first meeting, Notre Dame came to Falcon Stadium and beat the Air Force L (7-34). On Oct 17, Missouri beat the Air Force at home L (7–17). At Boston College on Oct 24, the Eagles owned the sky against the Falcons in Alumni Stadium, Chestnut Hill, MA L (7–13)

On Oct 31, at home, the Air Force beat Arizona W (7-0) . On Nov 7, at UCLA in Los Angeles Memorial Coliseum, Los Angeles, CA, the Falcons beat the Bruins in a nail-biter W (24–15). Then, on Nov 14 at home, Wyoming and the Air Force played to a tie match T (7-7). Then, on Nov 21, Colorado beat the Air Force at Colorado in Folsom Field, Boulder, CO., L (23–28)

1965 Air Force Falcons Coach Ben Martin

On Sep 18 in the season opener at Wyoming in War Memorial Stadium, Laramie, WY, the Cowboys defeated the Air Force L (14–31). On Sep 25 at home, #2 Nebraska beat Air Force L (17-27). On Oct 2, at home the Stanford Cardinal nosed out the Air Force Falcons L (16–17). On Oct 9 at home, California beat the Falcons L (7–24). On Oct 16 at Oregon's Multnomah Stadium in Portland, OR., the Ducks and the Falcons played to a tie T (18–18)

At Pacific on Oct 23 in Pacific Memorial Stadium in Stockton, CA, the Air Force lifted out of its funk and pummeled the Tigers W (40–0). On Oct 30 at home, UCLA shut out the Air Force Academy L (0–10). At Soldier Field in Chicago, Air Force defeated Army on Nov 6 W (14–3). On Nov 13 in Arizona Stadium, Tucson, AZ Air Force defeated Arizona W (34–7). Then, in the season close, at home, on Nov 20, Colorado beat the Falcons L (6–19)

1966 Air Force Falcons Coach Ben Martin

In the season and home opener on September 17, 1966 the Wyoming Cowboys shut out the Air Force Falcons in Falcon Stadium, Colorado Springs, CO. L (0–13). At Washington a week later on Sep 24 in a game played in Husky Stadium, Seattle, WA, the Falcons shut out the Huskies W (10–0) for the first win of the season. On Sep 31, Navy came to Falcon Stadium for the first time and were beaten for the first time by a feisty Air Force Squad that would not say no. W 15–7. At home on Oct8, the Falcons manhandled Hawaii W (54-0). Oregon got the best of Air Force on Oct 15 in a home game, defeating the Falcons L (6–17)

Colorado State kept the bad luck going with a victory over Air Force on Oct 22 at Falcon Stadium L (21–41. #3 ranked UCLA was having a fine year, ranked when the Bruins overpowered the Falcons at Los Angeles Memorial Coliseum, Los Angeles, CA L (13–38). At Stanford on Nov 5, the Cardinal defeated the Falcons in Stanford Stadium, Stanford, CA L 6–21. At North Carolina on Nov 12 in Kenan Memorial Stadium, Chapel Hill, NC, the Falcons beat the Tar Heels W (20–14). On Nov 19 at Colorado's Folsom Field in Boulder, the Buffaloes barely beat the Falcons L (9–10).

1967 Air Force Falcons Coach Ben Martin

In the season opener on September 16, 1967 at Oklahoma State, in a tough fought battle in Lewis Field, Stillwater, OK, the Cowboys and the Falcons fought to a scoreless tie T (0–0). On Sep 23, at Wyoming's War Memorial Stadium, Laramie, WY, the Cowboys beat the Falcons L (10–37) In the home opener on Sep 30, Washington beat the Falcons L (7–30). At California's Memorial Stadium in Berkeley, CA, on Oct 7, the Golden Bears edged out the Falcons L (12–14). On Oct 14, Air Force managed a win against North Carolina at home W (10-8)

At Tulane in Tulane Stadium , New Orleans, LA, the Falcons beat the Green Wave W (13–10). Colorado State then tied the Air Force on Oct 28 at home T (17–17). Army came to Falcon Stadium with both teams ready to play and the Black Knights emerged with the victory in a close match L (7–10). On Nov 11 at Arizona, the Wildcats defeated the Falcons L (10–14). Colorado then blanked the Falcons at home on Nov 18, L (0-33) to wrap up the Air Force season.

Chapter 6 Coach Ben Martin 1968-1977

Martin   Coach #3

Year	Coach	Record	Conference Record
1968	Ben Martin	7–3	Indep
1969	Ben Martin	6–4	Indep
1970	Ben Martin	9–3	Indep
1971	Ben Martin	6–4	Indep
1972	Ben Martin	6–4	Indep
1973	Ben Martin	6–4	Indep
1974	Ben Martin	2–9	Indep
1975	Ben Martin	2–8–1	Indep
1976	Ben Martin	4–7	Indep
1977	Ben Martin	2–8–1	Indep

Coach Ben Martin

In this chapter we look at the second half of Ben Martin's stint as the head coach of the Air Force Falcons. Martin had hist best season, undefeated at 9-0-2 year and his worst season, 2-6-2. He coached twenty years. In this Chapter we begin with his eleventh season which began a six-year clip of winning seasons before Martin's Air Force squad hit hard times again. His winning seasons included another 9-game winning season in 1970 when the Falcons went 9-3 and qualified for a bowl game for the second year in a row.

It helps to remember that when Martin became the coach at Air Force, he took over a fledgling football program, the academy's first class having entered in July 1955 at temporary facilities at Lowry Air Force Base in Denver. The football team had been coached by Buck Shaw during season 2 and 3.

I love to talk about Martin's first Air Force team, containing members of the academy's first senior class. These guys had the lean years and they waited their turn as seniors to bring in a bounty year for the Academy and for coach Ben Martin. You recall they went 9-0-1 in the regular season. Then, they played a 0-0 tie with Texas Christian in the Cotton Bowl, and this Ben Martin squad remains the only undefeated team in the academy's history.
You already know that one of Martin's teams also played in the 1963 Gator Bowl, losing to North Carolina. They also played in the 1971 Sugar Bowl, losing to Tennessee by 34-13.

Often featuring a short passing game, Martin had a career record of 96-103-9 at Air Force. After retiring as football coach, he was an analyst for ABC Sports, then was a radio analyst for Air Force football games from 1987 to 2002.

Martin was a native of Prospect Park, Pa., graduating in 1946 from the United States Naval Academy, where he played football and participated in track. He was prepared for his head coaching role at Air Force by having been an assistant football coach at Navy from 1949 to 1954. Then, before AFA, he was head football coach at the University of Virginia for two seasons.

1968 Air Force Falcons Coach Ben Martin

In the season opener on September 21at #6 Florida in Tampa Stadium, Tampa, FL, the Gators edged out the Falcons L (20–23). On

Sep 28 at home the Falcons beat Wyoming W (10–3). On Oct 5 at Stanford in Stanford Stadium, Stanford, CA, the Cardinal beat the Falcons, L (13–24). Then on Oct 12 in a game against Navy, played in Soldier Field, Chicago, IL, the Falcons outplayed the Midshipmen and carried home the victory W (26–20). On Oct 19 at Colorado State in Sonny Lubick Field at Hughes Stadium, Fort Collins, CO, the Falcons shut out the Cowboys W (31-0).

On Oct 26 at Pittsburgh in Pitt Stadium, Pittsburgh, PA, the Falcons defeated the Panthers W (27–14). At home on Nov 2, Air Force beat North Carolina W (28–15). At home again on Nov 9, Arizona edged out the Falcons L (10–14). Then, on Nov 16 at home Air Force beat Tulsa W (28–8). Then, on Nov 23 in Folsom Field, Boulder, CO, Colorado and Air Force engaged in a blowout where neither defense had bragging rights, but the Falcons came away with a high scoring victory W 58–35.

1969 Air Force Falcons Coach Ben Martin

In the season opener, the Air Force played SMU on September 13, 1969 in the Cotton Bowl Stadium, Dallas, TX. The Falcons got the win by edging out the Mustangs W (26–22). On Sept 20 at No. 10 Missouri in Memorial Stadium , Columbia, MO the Falcons hung on but were beaten L (17–19). At home on Sep 27, Wyoming edged out Air Force L (25–27). On Oct at North Carolina's Kenan Memorial Stadium in Chapel Hill, NC, the Falcons defeated the Tar Heels W (20–10). At home on Oct 18 Air Force pummeled Oregon in a blowout W (60–13).

On Oct 25 at home #20 ranked Air Force beat Colorado State W (28–7) . Then at Michie Stadium on Nov1, #19 Air Force, beat the Army W (13-6) in West Point, NY. On Nov 8, #19 Air Force at home defeated Utah State W (28–7) At #13 Stanford, the #20 ranked Air Force Academy slugged it out with the Cardinal but were defeated in the end in Stanford Stadium, Stanford, CA, on Nov 15, L (34–47) In a tough game against #8 Notre Dame on Nov 28 in Notre Dame Stadium, the House that Rockne Built, South Bend, IN, the Falcons almost beat the Fighting Irish L (6–13).

1970 Air Force Falcons Coach Ben Martin

This was the last season that Army was not on the Falcons' schedule; the Commander-in-Chief's Trophy was introduced two years later which matched the three academies annually. Previously, Air Force played Army in odd years and Navy in even years.

Bob Parker was the Falcon tossing the TDs this year. And, he tossed a lot of them. It was because of the passing of this great QB came the Falcons' notable wins over #9 Missouri, and #6 Stanford, led by Heisman Trophy winner Jim Plunkett. Stanford went on to upset #2 Ohio State in the Rose Bowl.

For the first time since the 1963 season, the Falcons appeared in a bowl game, but they lost by 21 points to #4 Tennessee in the Sugar Bowl in New Orleans on New Year's Day. The Volunteers were favored, and they jumped out to a 24–0 lead in the first quarter and the Falcons were not able to make up the difference.

The season and home opener was played on September 12, 1970 at Falcon Stadium in Colorado Springs, CO. The Falcons smothered Idaho W (45–7). On Sep 19 at Wyoming's War Memorial Stadium in Laramie, WY, the Falcons made it two in a row with a nice victory over the Cowboys W (41–17). At #9 Missouri, on Sep 26, the #20 ranked Falcons overpowered the Tigers at Busch Memorial Stadium in St. Louis, MO, W (37–14). Then, with three in a row, on Oct 3, #10 ranked Air Force 1 plowed through Colorado State at home W 37–22. At home and ranked # 8 nationally on Oct 10, undefeated with four wins in a row, the Air Force Falcons made quick work of Tulane's Green Wave on Oct 10, W (24–3)

With five wins in the Bank, the #7 ranked Falcons handily beat the Midshipmen on Oct 17 at Navy in RFK Stadium, Washington, D.C. W (26–3) It seemed nobody could touch the Falcons as they took on Boston College at home on Oct 24 and they had no problem putting away the Eagles W (35-10). Looking for eight in a row, on Oct 31, the #7 ranked Falcons got it by defeated Arizona in the first close match of the season at Arizona Stadium , Tucson, AZ W (23–20). Could this be another year for an undefeated season?

The answer came at Oregon on Nov 7 as the then ranked #9 Falcons lost in a tough contest with Oregon in Autzen Stadium, Eugene, OR L (35–46). The Falcons slid to #13 in the rankings as they hosted #6 ranked Stanford to Falcon Stadium and rebounded with a healthy win against the Cardinal W (31–14). Back up to #10 after the win at Stanford, the Falcons faced another defeat at the hands of the unranked Colorado Buffaloes at home L (19–49)

After a great season at 9-2-0, the Falcons were invited to the Sugar Bowl to play #4 ranked Tennessee in Tulane Stadium in New Orleans LA on New Year's Day, January 1, 1971. The Volunteers were a bit more on this day than the Falcons could handle L (13–34).

What a season!

1971 Air Force Falcons Coach Ben Martin

This was the last season that the Navy was not on the Falcons' schedule; the Commander-in-Chief's Trophy was introduced the following year which matched the three academies annually. Previously, Air Force played Navy in even years and Army in odd years.

The season and home opener was played on September 18, 1971 at Falcon Stadium in Colorado Springs, CO. The Falcons nosed out Missouri W (7–6). On Sep 25 at home, the Falcons beat Wyoming W (23–19). Then, on Oct 2 at #9 Penn State in Beaver Stadium, University Park, PA, the Nittany Lions edged out the Falcons L (14–16). Rolling along after the tough loss to PSU, at home, on Oct 9, the Air Force shut out SMU W (30–0). On Oct 16, at Falcon Stadium, AFA beat Army W (20–7).

October 23 at Colorado State's Hughes Stadium in Fort Collins, CO, the #20 ranked Falcons defeated the Rams W (17–12). On Oct 30, the test came against #13 Arizona State when the #18 Falcons gave it all and lost in Sun Devil Stadium, Tempe, AZ L (28–44). On Nov 6, at home a tough Oregon team beat the Falcons L (14-23). After such a good start, being in the rankings, the Falcons had fallen somewhat. What would they do the following week was the question?

The Falcons came back on Nov 13 at Tulsa in Skelly Stadium, Tulsa, OK and got the victory W 17–7. However, Colorado, the next opponent was preparing to spoil the fun. They did. On Nov 20, playing against a ranked #10 Colorado Buffaloes team at Folsom Field in Boulder, CO, the Falcons just could not keep up and ended its 1971 season on a loss L (17–53).

1972 Air Force Falcons Coach Ben Martin

This was first season for the Commander-in-Chief's Trophy. To anybody else but Army, Navy, and Air Force, the Trophy would not necessarily mean as much. However, from the time the terms for the trophy were announced all three service academies eagerly awaited the games in which they could compete for the Commander-in-Chief's Trophy. It is the most coveted trophy other than winning the Army-Navy game. Obviously, the AFA came along over sixty years after Army and Navy were competing. Perhaps when and if the Space Force comes to being, there will be a fourth team and then perhaps a series.

The rules for the Commander-in-Chief's Trophy are simple. It matches the three academies annually, and a winner is determined based on game outcomes. Previously, Air Force played Navy in even years and Army in odd years. The Falcons lost both games this year and then Army beat Navy in December to take the first title.

The season and home opener was played on September 16, 1972 at Falcon Stadium in Colorado Springs, CO. The Falcons blasted Wyoming out of the Park W (45-14). Then on Sep 23 at home, the Falcons whooped the Panthers W (41–13).

Nobody seemed to care that a fine team such as the Falcons were getting edged out or nosed out or otherwise but the Air Force Falcons themselves did care. They cared a lot but had nobody to take it out on. It should have been the Colorado Buffaloes they whooped on that particular day, but on Sept 30, 1972, the Falcons were playing the Wildcats from Davidson.

One of my buddies from Meyers High School, a great QB from Davidson, Rick Simonson, had just chosen to leave the school and come back to the home town to play for Wilkes-College. Maybe that was the reason the Falcons were so tough (Davidson had lost its QB) or perhaps Air Force had really gotten to be the tough team annually that coach Ben Martin had always wanted to have. Either way, on Sept 30, 1972, the Falcons were not accepting excuse slips and they shellacked the Davidson Wildcats team more than perhaps they should have. It all happened on Sept 30 at home in Falcon Stadium, Colorado Springs, CO. Air Force walked away with its biggest shutout victory ever W 68-6.

On Oct 7 at Colorado State, the Falcons, ranked at #19 played in Hughes Stadium , Fort Collins, CO, and they beat the Rams but good W 52–13. There was no doubt about the quality of that victory. The next week, the Falcons had to face another "always-tough" team, the Eagles of Boston College. Air Force was ranked # 16 at the time and this game was played on Oct 14 in BC's Alumni Stadium, Chestnut Hill, MA. The Falcons walked away with a really tough win W (13–9). It was a win, nonetheless.

As tough as Air Force knows how to play, Navy and Army have been playing just as tough--but a lot longer. Air Force never gives anything up on sentiment so on Oct 21 when Navy came into town to play at home in Falcon Stadium against #16 ranked Air Force, though they were unranked, no advantage was given to Navy. But, they won anyway! And they captured the first leg of the Commander-in-Chief's Trophy L (17–21). Such is life. My friends used to say that sometimes you eat the bear and sometimes the bear eats you. When that happens, it's over. Nonetheless, the season goes on.

On Oct 28 at # 16 Arizona State in Sun Devil Stadium in Tempe, AZ, despite being pushed back in its goals by Navy, the Falcons prevailed W (39–31). At Army, on Nov 4, the other half of the Commander-in-Chief's Trophy was the opponent at Michie Stadium in West Point, NY. Just like the Navy, the Army won by a few points L (14–17). The service games are the happiest to win but the saddest to lose.

Moving on to the toughest part of the AFA schedule, coming to Falcon Stadium were two national powerhouses that cared about nothing but winning. The first on Nov 12, was #12 a perennial ranked squad. In a bad year Notre Dame could even beat itself. On Nov 11, they were not playing themselves, they were playing the Falcons of the Air Force Academy at their home stadium. Tough as it was for both teams the game did end. On Nov 11 and the contender Notre Dame defeated the mighty Air Force at Falcon Stadium in Colorado Springs, CO L (7–21).

1973 Air Force Falcons Coach Ben Martin

The season and home opener was played on September 22, 1973 at Falcon Stadium in Colorado Springs, CO. The Falcons defeated Oregon W (24-17) On Sep 29 at home, the Falcons defeated New Mexico W (10–6). On Oct 6 at home, #7 Penn State defeated Air Force L (9–19). On Oct 13 at # 17 Colorado in Folsom Field, Boulder, CO, the Buffaloes defeated the Falcons L (17–38). On Oct 20 at Navy in a game played at the Navy–Marine Corps Memorial Stadium in Annapolis, MD for the Commander-in-Chief's Trophy, the Midshipmen dominated the Falcons L (6–42).

Playing Davidson on Oct 27, at home, the Falcons beat the Wildcats W (41–19). Air Force beat Army on Nov 3 at home while competing for the Commander-in-Chief's Trophy, W (43–10). On Nov 10, Air Force defeated Rutgers at home W (31–14). At #19 Arizona on Nov 17, the Falcons nosed out the Wildcats in Arizona Stadium, Tucson, AZ W (27–26). On Nov 22 in the final game of the 1973 season, while playing against #5 Notre Dame in Notre Dame Stadium, South Bend, IN, the Fighting Irish dominated play, defeating the Falcons L (15–48).

1974 Air Force Falcons Coach Ben Martin

Most football coaches will admit that there is a lot of luck involved in football game outcomes. There is no question that over all, the harder we work, the luckier we get, but with a small sample, we can have bad luck all day and not get any luckier. IMHO, Ben Martin's Falcons had an unlucky year. Look at the scores to the games. Six of the Falcon nine defeats in this season were decided by four or less points. That my friends, is why Ben Martin is still revered as a great coach. It was surely an unlucky year.

The season and home opener was played on September 14, 1974 at Falcon Stadium in Colorado Springs, CO. The Falcons pounded Idaho W (37-0). On Sep 21 at Oregon's Autzen Stadium in Eugene, OR, the Ducks defeated the Falcons by four L (23–27). At Wyoming on Sep 28 in War Memorial Stadium, Laramie, WY, the Cowboys defeated the Falcons by four L (16–20).

At home on Oct 5, Colorado nosed out Air Force for the win by one-point, L (27–28) At home against Tulane, on Oct 12, the Green Wave won by seven over the Falcons. On Oct 19 at home, Navy defeated Air Force by three points, W 19–16.

On Oct 26, v Rutgers in Rutgers Stadium, Piscataway, NJ, the Scarlet Knights defeated the Falcons by 17 points L (3–20). BYU then played the Falcons at home and won by two points L (10–12). On Nov 9 at Army's Michie Stadium in West Point, NY, the Black Knights beat the Air Force by one points L (16–17). On Nov 16 at home, Arizona beat the Falcons by three points L (24–27). When the Falcons played #5 Notre Dame in the last game of the year, they had had their fill of bad luck. So, this was not a close game as the Irish shutout the Falcons on Nov 23 at Notre Dame Stadium in South Bend, In L (0–38). This game was not a matter of luck.

1975 Air Force Falcons Coach Ben Martin

The season opener played on September 13, 1975 at Arkansas in the War Memorial Stadium in Little Rock, CO. The Falcons were pounded by Arkansas W (0--35). At Iowa State on September 20in Jack Trice Stadium, Ames, IA, the Falcons were defeated L (12–17 On Sep 27, Air Force tied #10 UCLA at home T (20–20). At RFK Stadium on Oct 4, vs. Navy in Washington, D.C. for the Commander-in-Chief's Trophy, the Midshipmen shut out the Falcons L (0–17). At BYU's LaVell Edwards Stadium • Provo, UT on Oct 11, the Falcons lost to the Cougars L (14–28). At home on Oct 18, Air Force came the closest to this point to beating #15 Notre Dame (one point) L (30–31)

On Oct 25, the Colorado State beat the Falcons in Hughes Stadium Fort Collins, CO L (10–47). On Nov 1 at home, the Air Force beat the Army W (33–3). On Nov 8 at Tulane in the Louisiana Superdome, New Orleans, LA, the Falcons beat the Green Wave by one-point W (13–12). At home on Nov 15, #15 California beat the Air Force Academy L (14–31). On Nov 23 at home, Wyoming beat Air Force L (10–24).

1976 Air Force Falcons Coach Ben Martin

The season and home opener was played on September 11, 1976 at Falcon Stadium in Colorado Springs, CO. The Falcons pounded

Pacific W (37-0). On Sept 25, #5 UCLA defeated Air Force in Rose Bowl Stadium Pasadena, CA L (7–40). At Kent State on Oct 2 at Kent State's Municipal Stadium Cleveland, OH, the Golden Flashes beat the Falcons L (19–24). Then, on Oct 9, at home in the battle for the Commander-in-Chief's Trophy, Air Force beat Navy W (13–3). Then, on Oct 16, at home the Air Force lost to Colorado State L (3–27). This year, even the citadel beat Air Force on Oct 23 L (7–26)

With the Commander-in-Chief's Trophy in their sights, the Falcons were defeated on Oct 30 at Army in Michie Stadium West Point, NY L (7–24). On Nov 6 at Arizona State in Sun Devil Stadium, Tempe, AZ, the Falcons lost by one-point W (31–30). On Nov 13 at Vanderbilt's Dudley Field in Nashville, TN, the Commodores beat the Falcons L (10–34). At home on Nov 20, Air Force beat Wyoming W (41–21).

1977 Air Force Falcons Coach Ben Martin

The season opener was played on September 10, 1977 at Wyoming War Memorial Stadium Laramie, WY. The Falcons and the Cowboys played to a scoreless tie. T (0-0) On Sep 17 at California in California Memorial Stadium, Berkeley, CA, the Golden Bears beat the Falcons L 14–24. At home on Sep 24, the Falcons beat Pacific in a close match W (15–13). At Georgia Tech on Oct 1 in Bobby Dodd Stadium • Atlanta, GA, the Yellow Jackets whooped the Falcons L (3–30). Then, on Oct 8 at Navy in Navy–Marine Corps Memorial Stadium • Annapolis, MD for the Commander-in-Chief's Trophy, the Midshipmen beat the Falcons L (7–10)

On Oct 15 at home, Arizona State beat Air Force L (14–37). On Oct 22 at Baylor in Floyd Casey Stadium , WAC, TX, the Air Force lost L(7–38). At home on Oct 29, Boston College defeated Air Force L (14–36). On Nov 5, at home, Army beat Air Force in a battle for the Commander-in-Chief's Trophy L (6–31). At home on Nov 12, Air Force defeated Vanderbilt W (34–28). In the season finale, on Nov 19, #6 Notre Dame defeated Air Force in a blowout at Notre Dame Stadium , South Bend, IN, L (0–49).

Ben Martin passes torch from the Hall of Fame

https://www.coloradosports.org/hall-of-fame/athletes/1978-inductees/ben-martin/

Ben Martin, the handsome Air Force Academy football mentor, is best noted for having established an excellent football program, for giving the academy a viable residence in the major college football neighborhood, and for consistently administrating at a first-class level. A native of Prospect Park, Pennsylvania, Martin attended Hill Preparatory School and Princeton University before his appointment to the Naval Academy in 1943. He started every varsity football game at Navy for three seasons as an end and halfback, and he graduated sixth in his class in 1946.

In 1949, Martin joined Eddie Erdelatz as assistant coach at Navy and in 1956 took over the head-coaching job at Virginia. Two years later, Martin replaced Buck Shaw at the Air Force Academy.

Martin was never able to match the unbeaten, 9-0-2, record his first AFA team accomplished in 1958 when the young academy fielded its first seniors. But he did bring credibility to the academy, and season after season he punctuated his schedule with remarkable upsets, including those over such powerhouses as UCLA, Nebraska, Colorado, Iowa, Oklahoma State, Army and many more.

By this time, the AFA was recognized as a companion academy with both Army and Navy, and Martin's football headlines did much to make this possible. People no longer asked, "What's an Air Force Academy?"

"I have a job to do", Martin said after being informed of the 1965 scandal that trimmed several blue-chip players off his roster. "Sure it's one of the biggest challenges of my life, but you've got to live a long time to run out of challenges."

Martin's twenty-year record at the Air Force Academy included ninety-six wins, 103 losses and nine ties. No deadlock was more surprising and did more to keynote his 1958 club than a 13-13 tie with the powerful Iowa. The Hawkeyes were forced to come from behind in the final two minutes.

Besides having the longest tenure of any coach in service academy history, Martin, in 1977, served as president of the American Football Coaches Association. Both were milestones in his career. In 1978, he was inducted into the Colorado Sports Hall of Fame.

One of the most astute public speakers in sports, Martin has authored two books on football, Ben Martin's Flexible-T Offense, and End Play. He also coached all-star teams in post-season competition, notably the North-South game and the East-West Shrine game in San Francisco.

During Martin's career, he was wooed by several other colleges and by professional teams in both the American and National Football Leagues. But Martin vowed he would never leave the academy. It was the only coaching job he wanted. Had he gone into the competitive area of college ranks with unlimited recruiting available, it is safe to say his won-lost record would rank with Woody Hayes, Bear Bryant and the other gridiron greats.

Chapter 7 Coach Bill Parcells 1978-1978

Parcells   **Coach #4**

Year	Coach	Record	Conference	Record
1978	Bill Parcells	3–8	Indep	

From the Denver Post

By IRV MOSS | imoss@denverpost.com |

PUBLISHED: August 13, 2013 at 2:52 pm | UPDATED: April 29, 2016 at 8:24 pm

A few days after Bill Parcells experienced what he called the ultimate reward from his life in football, he talked for a few minutes about the past.

The pleasure of being inducted into the Pro Football Hall of Fame was evident in his voice. He didn't stop to go over his career step by step, preferring to let the record speak for itself. Besides, the Super Bowl victories and other trophies earned along the way were secondary to his time at the podium Aug. 3 in Canton, Ohio.

"The Hall of Fame is the ultimate for me," Parcells said in a phone interview. "Winning Super Bowls were important pieces of the puzzle. Football has been a good life for me."

With all that big stuff, does he remember 1978, the year he spent as the head football coach at the Air Force Academy?

"That was a difficult year for me," Parcells said. "It was my first time as a head coach. I remember it."

Parcells took on the task of following Air Force coaching legend Ben Martin, who had become a coaching institution at Air Force. Martin had taken over the Falcons' program in 1958. His first team posted a 9-0-2 record, tying Iowa 13-13 during the regular season and tying TCU 0-0 in the Cotton Bowl.

The first Air Force team under the direction of Parcells won its first two games, both on the road, 34-25 at Texas-El Paso and 18-7 at Boston College. But they won only once more, against Kent State, to finish 3-8.

Parcells resigned and initially planned to move to the staff of the New England Patriots. However, he turned down the job in New England and remained in Colorado Springs and out of coaching for a year.

"The year away from football was a difficult part of my life," Parcells explained, without offering a reason why he stayed away. A report at the time stated it was for family reasons.

Even though Parcells' time was short at Air Force, he left his mark. He generally is credited with persuading the command at Air Force of the value of an organized weight training program. Jack Braley was a carryover from Martin's staff and a proponent of the value of weight training. Braley remains with the program today.

Former basketball coach Hank Egan remembers something that might have been even more important.

"One of the things Bill did was to hire a bunch of young assistant coaches," Egan said. "That group started a change in the culture and the philosophy at the academy. Ken Hatfield was in the group."

Hatfield followed Parcells as Air Force's head coach. During his term, Air Force joined the Western Athletic Conference and adopted the wishbone offense that became the bread-and-butter for the Falcons. Parcells stepped into a job that was much different from what he expected.

"I had been an assistant coach at Army before taking the job at Air Force," he said. "I had an idea what I was getting into. But it was different from what I expected. I understood the mission of the academy, but I had difficulty understanding what they wanted from their athletic teams."

Parcells won two Super Bowls with the New York Giants, the first coming with a 39-20 triumph over the Broncos in January 1987. Overall, Parcells posted a 172-130-1 NFL record in 22 seasons while coaching the Giants, Patriots, New York Jets and Dallas Cowboys.

"I'm happy the way everything turned out," Parcells said. "I'd never go back in. I'm at the age (72 this month) where that wouldn't be a good idea. I am fortunate to have been with good people and organizations that supported me."

Irv Moss: 303-954-1296, imoss@denverpost.com or twitter.com/irvmoss

A little more on Parcells – good stuff

Parcells: It all started in Colorado Springs
https://www.csindy.com/coloradosprings/parcells-it-all-started-in-colorado-springs/Content?oid=2625013

End Zone
By Ralph Routon
…

Many will call it foolish to suggest that Bill Parcells, just named to the Pro Football Hall of Fame, should think of Colorado Springs as the turning point of his remarkable coaching career. But they don't know Parcells' story.

It's true that Parcells had been an assistant at five schools, including Florida State and Texas Tech, before coming to Air Force as head coach in 1978, replacing the legendary Ben Martin. But his time in the Springs set the stage for Parcells becoming one of the National Football League's most influential figures.

Only a few head coaches can claim two Super Bowl rings (with the New York Giants) and other playoff experiences, making history during 20-plus years of running the show with such famed franchises as New York's Giants and Jets, the New England Patriots, Dallas Cowboys and finally, as an executive, the Miami Dolphins.

But none of that would have happened if not for Parcells' experiences here, as he has admitted on several occasions. He thought he would become a big-time college coach, but that dream ended at the academy — and actually led him to consider other options locally before embracing the NFL.

...

Just a few weeks before 1979 spring practice, Parcells suddenly accepted a job as a defensive assistant for the Giants. Hatfield took over at Air Force, adding to that staff such later-recognizable names as Chan Gailey and Fisher DeBerry, and led the Falcons toward what has become three decades of near-constant success.

But that wasn't the end of Parcells' time here. When he bolted from Air Force, his wife and kids stayed here to finish that school year. They didn't want to leave, and within a few months, Parcells was back again, leaving the Giants before training camp and returning to Colorado Springs as what he later would call "athletic director" at Gates Land Co. and the Country Club of Colorado.

During that 1979 season, Parcells moonlighted doing commentary for local high school football broadcasts on KRDO-AM. He would come to the Garry Berry Stadium press box, wearing an overcoat with a flask inside to spice up the hot chocolate or coffee, and we'd talk football at all levels. Fascinating, to say the least.

His family was happy, but he wasn't. So when the NFL called again in 1980, Parcells was gone to New England for a year, then to the Giants. He became their head coach in 1983, and the rest is history.

Parcells never forgot Colorado Springs. Whenever we've bumped into each other, he's stopped to reminisce. He always felt proud of that AFA staff he assembled, and he singled out players such as quarterback Dave Ziebart, linebacker Tom Foertsch and defensive end Dave Scott. To Parcells, those Falcons' commitment and spunk put them right alongside NFL stars he coached, from Lawrence Taylor and Phil Simms to Curtis Martin, Keyshawn Johnson and more.

Where would Bill Parcells have gone if he hadn't spent those two years in Colorado Springs? We'll never know, but we do know that he left here determined to succeed at football's highest level —which is exactly what he did. — routon@csindy.com

1978 Air Force Falcons Coach Bill Parcells

The season opener was played on September 9, 1979 against UTEP at the Sun Bowl in El Paso, TX. The Falcons pounded the Miners W (34-25). At BC on Sep 16 in Alumni Stadium, Chestnut Hill, MA, the Falcons won their second game in a row—this one against the BC Eagles W (18–7). At home, on Sep 23, Holy Cross defeated the Air Force L (18–35). At Kansas State, on Sep 30, at KSU Stadium in Manhattan, KS, the Wildcats beat the Falcons L (21–34). On Oct 7, at home, Navy beat Air Force as part of the competition for the Commander-in-Chief's Trophy L (8–37). On Oct 14, at home, Colorado State defeated Air Force L (13–31).

At home, on Oct 21, #18 Notre Dame beat Air Force L (15–38). Then, on Oct 28 at home, Air Force defeated Kent State W (26–10). On Nov. 4, playing Army as part of the Commander in Chief's competition in Michie Stadium, West Point, NY the Black Knights defeated the Falcons L (14–28). On Nov 1, at home, #19 Georgia Tech beat the Air Force L (21–42). For the season finale, on Nov 18 at Vanderbilt in Vanderbilt Stadium , Nashville, TN, the Commodores defeated the Falcons L (27–41).

Chapter 8 Coach Ken Hatfield 1979-1983

Hatfield   **Coach #5**

Year	Coach	Record	Conference	Record
1979	Ken Hatfield	2–9		
1980	Ken Hatfield	2–9–1	WAC	1–3
1981	Ken Hatfield	4–7	WAC	2–3
1982	Ken Hatfield	8–5	WAC	4–3
1983	Ken Hatfield	10–2	WAC	5–2

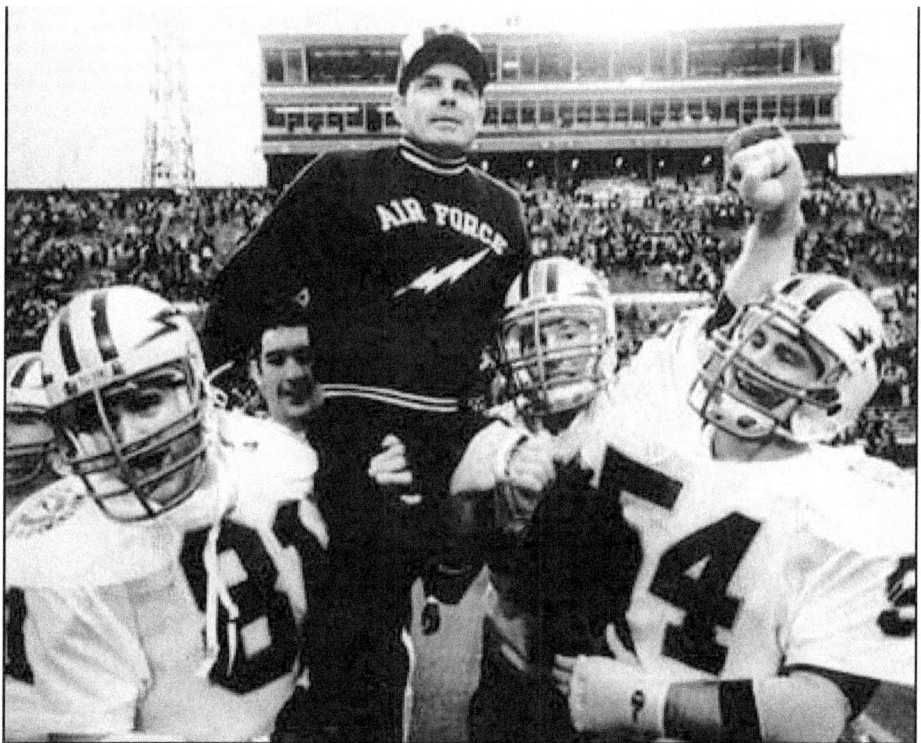

Air Force soared to new heights in the early 1980s under Ken Hatfield, posting two bowl wins, the first over Vanderbilt in the 1982 Hall of Fame Bowl. Now 63 and living in Houston, his last game at Air Force was the 1983 Independence Bowl, a win over Ole Miss.

Making most of options (Irv's title)

Bill Parcells hired Ken Hatfield as a young assistant in his one-year at AFA in 1978. He also indirectly hired Fisher DeBerry who will get a lot of press in this book soon after Mr. Hatfield. There are no McCoys in either story, but we can't swear that there are not some relationships in the past. These two acts of Parcells alone kept Air Force on the map—yes, the big US football map after the Ben Martin years.

We have a saying in Scranton PA that goes like this: "Nothing happens overnight in Scranton." Let the saying go as it is because it applies to a lot of life situations that require time. Impatient creatures that humans are, often we are not willing to give time to gearing up to win. We just want to win. It is a human fault. We just want to win. The Rolling Stones, not known as modern day philosophers got it right in the song, in fact, right in the title, "You can't always get what you want." True in football, true in life.

Even "the Tuna" could not turn AFA around in one year but he tried. You can't always get what you want but then again, nothing in life worth having is easy. By the way, it was with the Pats that Parcells earned the nickname "BigTuna." Said Parcells, "the players pulled a practical joke and I said, 'Do you think I'm Charlie the Tuna, like a sucker?' After that, they called me Tuna. "Apr 1, 2014

So when Ken Hatfield noticed Air Force was not Army or Navy, and that his mentor Bill Parcells won just three games, he knew life could not be easy as head coach to turn a big over-officered program around. But, kids think they can do anything. Hatfield finally got enough time to get the job done without being fired. DeBerry, when he became miffintiff, had Hatfield's legacy to lean on as he gained more and more prominence within the Air Force Hierarch (i.e. the bosses)

Irv Moss, of the Denver Post has written magnificent pieces about the Air Force Falcons. The following is another one of them. Thank you, Irv Moss, for sharing your work with us all:

https://www.denverpost.com/2006/10/15/making-most-of-options/

"When Ken Hatfield thinks back to 1979 and his first season as football coach at Air Force, he can't help but remember having a sense of urgency.

It wasn't that he was anticipating a bowl bid. Far from it. He knew his team would struggle and it did, starting 0-8, with a 13-9 loss to Navy as close as the Falcons would come in the first two months.

"I thought I was going to get fired in a hurry," Hatfield recalled. But he had the full support of Air Force athletic director John Clune.

"I think (he) kept me alive and on the job," said Hatfield, who had ascended to head coach at a time when the academy's football program was in a state of turmoil. Ben Martin had retired after the 1977 season after 20 years at the helm, with his last four teams posting losing records.

Bill Parcells replaced Martin in 1978 but stayed only one season, going 3-8. Hatfield was the offensive coordinator under Parcells and was elevated to head coach when he left.

But after eight games, it appeared there was little to be hopeful about. In the ninth game, the Falcons played Army, then coached by Lou Saban. Hatfield put in some running plays specifically designed for quarterback Dave Ziebart and Air Force upset Army, 28-7, to end an 11-game losing streak.

But more important, Ziebart's performance added fuel to Hatfield's growing realization that revamping Air Force's offense was the way of the future. He knew it would be a controversial decision, but he decided to introduce the triple option wishbone attack full time the following season.

"John Clune came to me and asked if I really was going to run a new offense," Hatfield said. "He said a lot of Air Force alumni weren't going to be happy."

Hatfield invited Jim Brakefield, a proponent of the option at Appalachian State, to come to the academy and talk to his staff.

Brakefield brought his coaching staff to Colorado Springs, including Fisher DeBerry, whom Hatfield later hired prior to the 1980 season to help install the attack.

As Hatfield pondered changing his offense, another major step was taken that would greatly influence Air Force football. The Falcons joined the Western Athletic Conference for the 1980 season.

One of the factors in Hatfield making the move was the ability of a service academy to attract triple option quarterbacks.

"Our first goal was to beat Army and Navy and I knew they weren't playing anybody who ran the option," Hatfield said. "In our recruiting, we knew that good option quarterbacks didn't have a lot of other places to go."

When Hatfield departed Air Force after the 1983 season to coach Arkansas, his alma mater, DeBerry was promoted to the head coaching spot and the legacy prospered.

"The decision to join a conference and the decision to use the option offense are the two biggest reasons for what our football program has become," DeBerry said. "Ken made the right decision to bring in the option offense and Gen. (Kenneth) Tallman and John Clune made the right decision to put us in a conference."

DeBerry looks at a 21-16 victory over San Diego State in 1981 in the Mirage Bowl in Tokyo as a benchmark victory. The following year, the Falcons beat BYU for the first time, 39-38, with quarterback Marty Louthan running the option in a game that became a part of WAC football lore. That year, the Falcons also defeated Army and Navy for the first time in the same season en-route to winning its first Commander-in-Chief's Trophy.

But maybe the most memorable victory that season was a 30-17 triumph over Notre Dame, the first of four consecutive victories against the Irish. DeBerry's 12-1 team completed the run in 1985.

Hatfield's best team was his last, the team that went 10-2 in 1983. The Colorado Springs Sports Hall of Fame is honoring Hatfield and that team at its Oct. 25 banquet at the World Arena.

"Everything that was happening was kind of a first," Hatfield said.

"You didn't know how to handle it because it was all new." Hatfield's last game as Air Force coach was a 9-3 victory over Mississippi in the 1983 Independence Bowl. His coaching stops later took him to Arkansas, Clemson and Rice, with whom he parted ways after last season, his 12th as Owls coach. Hatfield, 63, lives in Houston and said he doesn't know if he'll coach again.

"More than likely I won't coach again, but you never know," Hatfield said.

Zooming higher

Ken Hatfield's coaching record in five seasons at Air Force:
1979 2-9-0
1980 2-9-1
1981 4-7-0
1982 8-5-0
1983 10-2-0

Totals 26-32-1

Irv Moss is a great writer. Thank you Irv. Mr. Moss can be reached at 303-954-1296 or imoss@denverpost.com. What a guy!

1979 Air Force Falcons Coach Ken Hatfield

Air Force finished the season outscored by their opponents 127–253; the Falcons lost their first eight games, but finished by winning two of their last three, finishing 2–9.

The season and home opener was played on September 8, 1979 against Tulsa at home in Falcon Stadium, Colorado Springs, CO. The Falcons were semi-pounded by the Golden Hurricane L (7-24). On Sep 15 at Wisconsin in Camp Randall Stadium Madison, WI, the Falcons took it on the chin L (0–38). On Sep 22 v Illinois at home, the Fighting Illini beat the Falcons L (19–27). Then, on Sep 29, at home, Kansas State defeated the Air Force L (6–19). Navy came in again to Falcon Stadium with guns a-blazing. They coveted as all service academies, the Commander-in-Chief's Trophy. They overcame the desire of Air Force for the same trophy and beat the Falcons on Oct 6, L (7–24).

On Oct 13, at home, #10Notre Dame soundly defeated the Falcons L (13–38). Then, on Oct 20 at Oregon's Autzen Stadium in Eugene, OR, the Ducks prevailed L (9–17). At Colorado State, on Oct 27 in Sonny Lubick Field at Hughes Stadium in Fort Collins, CO, the Rams prevailed L (6–20). Then, on Nov 3, at home, Army took its crack at the Commander-in-Chief's Trophy), but with a specially designed Ken Hatfield offense the Black Knights did not know what hit them in defeat W (28–7). At Georgia Tech on Nov 10 at Bobby Dodd Stadium in Atlanta, Georgia, the Yellow Jackets shut out the Falcons L (0–21). In the season finale, on Nov 17 at home, Vanderbilt was nosed out and the Air Force prevailed W (30–29).

The season opener was played on September 6, 1980 against Colorado State in Hughes Stadium, Fort Collins, CO for the Ram–Falcon Trophy. The Falcons lost L (9–21). On Sep 13 at Washington's Husky Stadium in Seattle, WA, the Huskies walloped the Falcons L (7–50). On Sep 20 at home, San Diego State beat the Falcons L (10–13). At Illinois' Memorial Stadium in Champaign, IL, the Fighting Illini tied the Falcons T (20-20). On Oct 4 at Yale in the Yale Bowl stadium in New Haven, CT, the Bulldogs nosed out the Falcons L (16–17). For the Commanders in Chief game on Oct 11 at home, the Air Force nosed out Navy W (21-20), putting them in line for a possible trophy.

On Oct 18 at Tulane in the Louisiana Superdome, New Orleans, LA, the Green Wave beat the Falcons L (7–28). Then, at home, Boston College shut out the Air Force on Nov 1 L (0–23). The notion of winning the Commander in Chief Trophy was at the top of the Air Force squad's minds as they entered Michie Stadium in West Point, NY. Despite the tough play in this game on Nov 8, Army had just enough juice to squeak out a victory over the Air Force L (24–47) After a tough loss, the Air Force came right back the next week on Nov 16, and they beat Wyoming well, at home W 25–7.

Notre Dame was no longer able to look at Air Force as an easy mark, even though the Falcons had yet to prevail in the series. In this game played on Nov 22, Notre Dame prevailed in Notre Dame Stadium, South Bend, IN L (10–24). Since it is always warm in Hawaii, and Pearl Harbor is a US base, the Falcons got a weather-breather but not a game-breather on Nov 29, in Aloha Stadium, Honolulu, HI as the Rainbow Warriors came out on top against the Falcons L (12–20).

1981 Air Force Falcons Coach Ken Hatfield

The season opener was played on September 12, 1981 against BYU in Cougar Stadium, Provo, UT. The Falcons turned in another highly unsuccessful opening day L (21-45). On Sep 19, at home, Wyoming barely beat the Air Force in Falcon Stadium in the home opener L (10–17). At New Mexico on Sep 26 in New Mexico University Stadium, Albuquerque, NM, the Lobos defeated the Falcons L (10–27).

Looking for a win, Air Force found it on Oct 3 at home v Colorado State and the Falcons picked up the Ram–Falcon Trophy in a nice win W (28–14). On Oct 10, Navy emerged as the candidate for the Commander in Chief's Trophy in a game played at Navy–Marine Corps Memorial Stadium, Annapolis, MD. L (13-30).

On Oct 17, at home, the Tulane Green Wave got its dander up and defeated the Falcons L (13–31) On Oct 24 at Oregon, in Autzen Stadium in Eugene, OR, the Falcons picked up the W, W (20–10). After ruining a clean Commander's trophy in 1980 for the AFA, the Falcons made the Army pay in this great game played at home on Oct 31 at home as the Falcons preyed on the Black Knights in a low-scoring encounter in which the Falcons prevailed W (7–3).

Notre Dame, impervious to the Air Force improvements, came in as usual and on Nov 14, the Fighting Irish again defeated the Falcons at home L 7–35. On Nov 21 at UNLV, in a game played at the Las Vegas Silver Bowl in Las Vegas, NV, the Falcons almost won but lost to the Rebels L (21–24). In the season finale, on Nov 28 v San Diego State in National Olympic Stadium, Tokyo, Japan in a game labeled as the Mirage Bowl, the Falcons triumphed W 21–16

1982 Air Force Falcons Coach Ken Hatfield

The AF squad was selected to play in the Hall of Fame Classic, in which it defeated Vanderbilt 36–28.

The season opener was played on September 4, 1982 against Tulsa in Skelly Stadium, Tulsa, OK. The Falcons turned in fine effort for opening day but a loss nonetheless L (17-35). On Sep 11, at home, San Diego State was defeated soundly by Air Force W (44–32). Looking for wins and not just close encounters of the unkind kind, Air Force met the latter on Sep 18 at Texas Tech in Clifford B. and Audrey Jones Stadium, Lubbock, TX, and the Falcons lost literally by a nose hair L (30–31). At BYU, on Sep 25, in Cougar Stadium, Provo, UT, the Falcons luck had turned as the squad literally nosed out the Cougars W 39–38.

At home on Oct 2, New Mexico got the best of Air Force L (37–49) in a tough match. At home again, in Falcon Stadium, for the Commander in Chief's award, the Air Force defeated the Navy in a real tussle W (24–21). In another tough game at home, on Oct 16, Colorado State beat the Falcons L (11–21). Then, on Oct 23, at UTEP, in a game played in the Sun Bowl of El Paso, TX, the Falcons came alive and prevailed W (35–7).

On Oct 30 at home, the Falcons defeated Wyoming W (44–34). Then, on Nov 6, the Air Force for the first time captured the Commander-in Chief's Trophy) in a great victory over Army W (27-9) The Air Force Academy Football Team had arrived.

To have a really good year, Air Force had to beat a team for the first time, such as Notre Dame. Could they do it? Yes, they could! Here's how. On Nov 20, though Notre Dame came in to Falcon Stadium in the top 20 (18), the Falcons, coached by Ken Hatfield, were ready and they blew the Irish out of the park--W (30–17). Go Air Force.

Then on Nov 27 at Hawaii in Aloha Stadium, Honolulu, HI , the Air Force was still celebrating their ND victory and the lost L (21–45). By December 31 (New Year's Eve), playing in the Holiday Hall of Fame Classic against Vanderbilt in Legion Field, Birmingham, AL, the Air Force Falcons won their first Bowl Game W (36–28). Go Air Force.

1983 Air Force Falcons Coach Ken Hatfield

After waiting three years for positive results from coach Hatfield, the time had come, and he delivered in 1982 and he delivered again this year in 1983. Air Force had left its funk in 1982 and they renewed their former excellence on the field. Coach Hatfield's patience had paid off. In Ken Hatfield's last year, Air Force was delivering and with Fisher DeBerry coming up next, the Falcons years never shone so bright.

The bad luck streak was over. The team finished the regular season with a phenomenal 9–2 overall record and a 5–2 record in the Western Athletic Conference games. The team was selected to play in the Independence Bowl, in which it defeated another long-term great team, Ole Miss 9–3

The season opener was played on September 3, 1983 against Colorado State in Hughes Stadium, Fort Collins CO for the RAM-Falcon trophy The Falcons turned in a fine effort for opening day, defeating Colorado State W (34-13). At home on Sep 10, Air Force defeated Texas Tech W (28–13). At Wyoming's War Memorial Stadium in Laramie, WY, the Cowboys edged out the Falcons L (7–14). Then, at home, on Sept BYU put it all together to whip the Falcons L (28-46). This would be the last loss of the season and the first year in which Air Force won all the marbles for the Commander-in-Chief's Trophy. On Oct 8 at Navy's Marine Corps Memorial Stadium in Annapolis, MD, the Falcons pounded the Midshipmen W (44–17).

At home with UTEP on Oct 15, the Falcons defeated the Miners W (37–25). Then, on Oct at home again, the Falcons nosed out Utah W (33–31). At home on Oct 29, Air Force solidified the Commander-in-Chief's Trophy by defeating the Army W (41–20). At home, on Nov 5, the Falcons pounded Hawaii W (45–10). At ND, on Nov 19, Air Force enjoyed its first-ever victory over Notre Dame at Notre Dame Stadium in South Bend, IN as the Falcons nosed out the Fighting Irish W (23–22).

At San Diego State on Nov 26, the #18 ranked Air Force Squad defeated the Aztecs at Jack Murphy Stadium • San Diego, CA W 38–7. Ranked #16 for the Season Finale, on Dec 10, the Falcons edged out Ole Miss at Independence Stadium, Shreveport, LA W (9–3).

The Independence Bowl

For the Second year in a row with Ken Hatfield, the Falcons made it to a bowl game. This year's game was early on Dec 10 and the Air Force took on the Rebels of Mississippi. The Rebs had tied for third place in their Southeastern Conference. It was their first bowl encounter since 1971.

The Falcons had another good year and had gained the #2 spot in the Western Athletic Conference right behind BYU, who had defeated the Falcons in the regular season. This was the Falcons 2nd straight bowl game. It marked the first time Air Force had made consecutive bowl games in school history. This was the first Independence Bowl in which either team competed.

The game conditions were a ton less than ideal with rain and a drenching as the order of the day. The Air Force got the lead at 6-0 on two field goals by Sean Pavlich from 44 and 39 yards out. Ole Miss cut this in half on a 39-yard field goal from Neil Teevan in the 3rd, but then Falcons' Pavlich's 27 yarder in the same quarter proved to be the last score of the game.

QB Marty Louthan was 6-of-7 for 71 yards, and Buford McGee rushed 22 times for 111 yards for the Falcons. In a losing effort for the Rebels, Mike Brown ran for 91 yards on 12 carries. Kelly Powell threw 11-of-27 for 138 yards, with 2 interceptions. The Air Force picked up its second bowl win in two years.

Dec 22, 1983, Ken Hatfield Leaves AFA for Arkansas

We thank UPI for this article from their archives

FAYETTEVILLE, Ark.

Ken Hatfield, formerly football coach at the Air Force Academy, Thursday was named coach at the University of Arkansas. The move ended a four-day search that began Sunday with the unexpected resignation of Lou Holtz.

The announcement was made by Arkansas athletic director Frank Broyles after a meeting with university officials. Broyles stated earlier he would wait until after the Jan. 2 bowl games to announce a choice but said Thursday the 'situation was too volatile' to wait that long.

Hatfield was at Fayetteville Tuesday and Wednesday and described his visit as an 'information-gathering' effort. At the time he said the job had not been offered and he was not sure he would accept it if it were. Sources said Hatfield was being pressured by Air Force officials to let them know of his intentions.

Hatfield, a native Arkansan, will be returning to the school where he led the nation in punt returns as co-captain of Broyles' 1964 national championship team.

'This is a great day for the University of Arkansas and for Razorbacks fans everywhere,' Broyles said in announcing the appointment. 'Under Ken Hatfield's leadership, the future of our football program will be all we want it to be,' he said.

'Arkansas fans have taken tremendous pride in Ken Hatfield's accomplishments at the Air Force Academy. This high opinion of him does not stop here. Just this week, I have been told by some of the most prominent coaches and athletic directors in the nation that he is the best young coach in the country. His achievements cannot be overestimated.'

Thursday, Holtz accepted the head coaching position at the University of Minnesota. He announced at a tense news conference Sunday that he was 'tired and burned out' and was stepping down at Arkansas for 'personal reasons' that he declined to discuss.

The Razorbacks' 6-5 finish this year was the worst in Holtz's seven seasons at Arkansas. Four of his assistants were either fired or resigned at season's end, and Holtz came under pressure for making campaign commercials endorsing conservative Sen. Jesse Helms, R-N.C.

Meanwhile, Hatfield's Air Force team was wrapping up a 10-2 campaign, marking the first time since 1905 that the Falcons had won as many as 10 games in a season. Until last year's 8-5 mark, the Falcons had endured five straight losing seasons, and Hatfield was recognized generally as the biggest factor in the turnaround.

From the time Holtz resigned, Hatfield -- along with three other successful head coaches who played under Broyles at Arkansas -- was mentioned prominently. He was the first and one of only two of those coaches to visit the campus, departing just as Oklahoma State's Jimmy Johnson arrived Wednesday.

Texas' Fred Akers and Oklahoma's Barry Switzer declined Broyles' offer to discuss the position. Tulsa's John Cooper also had been mentioned, but he was never contacted by Broyles.

'It is ironic that Kenny and I have had virtually no personal contact in the 19 years since he left the University of Arkansas,' Broyles said. 'However, after visiting with Ken this week, it is obvious he possesses the strong qualities which have made him successful. Not only is he a warm, caring and concerned person, but he has the mental toughness which is needed for success in this demanding profession.

'These are the key reasons he is so highly regarded by his peers everywhere. With all this, it is wonderful to realize that he is a native Arkansan, a former captain of the Razorbacks, an All-America player, president of his senior class, brigade commander of his ROTC unit and an outstanding student. We can all look forward confidently to the future under his leadership.'

Broyles said Hatfield would hold a news conference Monday at Fayetteville.

Read more: https://www.upi.com/Archives/1983/12/22/Ken-Hatfield-formerly-football-coach-at-the-Air-Force/6865440917200/#ixzz5d4C07xqR

Chapter 9 Coach Fisher DeBerry 1984-1995
Part 1 1984 to 1995

DeBerry   Coach # 6

Year	Coach	Record	Conf	Record
1984	Fisher DeBerry	8–4	WAC	4–3
1985	Fisher DeBerry	12–1	WAC	7–1
1986	Fisher DeBerry	6–5	WAC	5–2
1987	Fisher DeBerry	9–4	WAC	6–2
1988	Fisher DeBerry	5–7	WAC	3–5
1989	Fisher DeBerry	8–4–1	WAC	5–1–1
1990	Fisher DeBerry	7–5	WAC	3–4
1991	Fisher DeBerry	10–3	WAC	6–2
1992	Fisher DeBerry	7–5	WAC	4–4
1993	Fisher DeBerry	4–8	WAC	1–7
1994	Fisher DeBerry	8–4	WAC	6–2
1995	Fisher DeBerry	8–5	WAC	6–2

About Coach DeBerry

Fisher DeBerry had a long coaching career by the time he got the head coaching job at Air Force. Reading bio tracks and great articles over the years about DeBerry, he was so significant for Air Force, it might appear to the uninformed that he was born and then he became the Air Force Coach as Air Force is where his prominence as a person and as a coach was really highlighted.

Like many great legendary head coaches before and after him, however, DeBerry spent his requisite time in the low-level jobs before emerging in the big time. For DeBerry, who was born in Cheraw, South Carolina in 1938, his sports affiliation began as a four-sport varsity letter winner. Name the Sport and he was a star—not just a player—a star. He even lettered , five times in baseball. Add to that his three letters each in football and basketball and two in track, and you have one heck of a sports figure before he got out of high school.

He was also all-state in baseball and football. DeBerry. After HS, he went to Wofford College in Spartanburg, South Carolina. Again, he lettered in football and baseball. He graduated in 1960. And pre-graduation had time to be active in the Kappa Sigma Fraternity while in college. Think about that for awhile

Kappa Sigma's are taught to live their lives by the symbols of the Star and Crescent, these symbols of the Fraternity make up the official badge:
The Star and Crescent shall not be worn by every man, but only by him who is worthy to wear it.

The Kappa Signa Fraternity seems like a natural place for a guy with the great talents of a Fisher DeBerry, does it not?

- He must be a gentleman
- a man of honor and courage
- a man of zeal, yet humble
- an intelligent man ...
- a man of truth ...
- one who tempers action with wisdom and,
- above all else, one who walks in the light of God.

After graduation, DeBerry stuck around while teaching and coaching high school sports. He went back to his alma mater, Wofford and coached college for the first time (2 years). While there as an assistant, Wofford won 21 consecutive games and was ranked first in the NAIA. From 1971 to 1979, DeBerry took his talents to Appalachian State for those nine years.

Again. While DeBerry did his thing there, it paid off as usual. Appalachian State was ranked in the top 10 nationally in those years in either rushing, total offense, or scoring offense three times. In 1974, the team was ranked sixth nationally in pass defense when he was operating as defensive coordinator. His legacy is long before his legacy even began.

He was noticed by Ken Hatfield who gave him the call. And as they say in the old country, the rest is history. Let's look at this UPI article about the time when DeBerry got the call to become head coach of the Air Force.

Offensive coordinator of the Air Force Academy...

(0)

AIR FORCE ACADEMY, Colo. -- Fisher DeBerry, offensive coordinator of the Air Force Academy football team the past several years, Tuesday was named head coach of the Falcons.

DeBerry signed a four-year contract, effective immediately.

DeBerry, 45, succeeds Ken Hatfield, who last week was named head coach at the University of Arkansas. Hatfield said following his appointment that he would name DeBerry his offensive coordinator at Arkansas if academy officials did not make him his successor.

'We are delighted he has accepted the position,' Athletic Director Col. John Clune said at a news conference. 'He knows the academy and what our program represents. I feel the academy football program is in excellent hands and I'm looking forward to working with him to maintain the momentum in our program which has been established over the last five years.'

DeBerry said he hoped to continue the winning traditional established under Hatfield's leadership, which included Falcon appearances in the 1982 Hall of Fame bowl game and in the 1983 Independence Bowl. 'I appreciate the confidence the Air Force staff has in my abilities and this had been the best Christmas gift that anybody ever had,' he said. 'It's a dream come true as it's always a goal for an assistant to become head coach.

DeBerry said although the academy was losing 23 seniors next June, he was confident of fielding a competitive squad.

The Falcons defeated Notre Dame the past two seasons and finished their 1983 campaign with a 10-2 record.

DeBerry, a 1960 graduate of Wofford College in Spartanburg, S.C., joined the academy's coaching staff in March 1980 as quarterback coach and served the next three years as offensive coordinator.

Previously he served as defensive and offensive coordinator at Appalachian State in North Carolina.

Read more: https://www.upi.com/Archives/1983/12/27/Fisher-DeBerry-offensive-coordinator-of-the-Air-Force-Academy/4458441349200/#ixzz5d4QIgvqF

DeBerry had a great career at Air Force. Next June, he will mark his 81st birthday. With a full name of James Fisher DeBerry, he was born June 8, 1938. You will learn that he served as the head football coach at the United States Air Force Academy from 1984 to 2006, compiling a compelling record of 169–109–1. He has a phenomenal record of coaching accomplishments.

DeBerry led 17 of his 23 Air Force Falcons squads to winning records and captured 12 bowl game bids. Three times his teams won the Western Athletic Conference title, in 1985, 1995, and 1998. DeBerry retired on December 15, 2006 with the most wins and highest winning percentage (.608) in Air Force football history. He was inducted into the College Football Hall of Fame as a coach in 2011.

Many have heard Ken Hatfield's story of hiring DeBerry in 1980 as the Air Force Academy quarterbacks coach. The next year, he promoted him to offensive coordinator. In 1982, under Hatfield, Air Force posted an 8-5 record while averaging 30.4 points per game. The AFA beat Vanderbilt in the 1982 Hall of Fame Classic. After the 1983 season, Hatfield left Air Force for Arkansas after the Falcons' 10-2 season and Independence Bowl victory. DeBerry was promoted to head coach.

Air Force won at least eight games 11 different seasons during DeBerry's tenure as head coach. His first team, in 1984, after having lost most of the team in the prior year, was 8–4 and the Falcons beat Virginia Tech in the 1984 Independence Bowl.

The next year, the Falcons killed it all, winning 12 games. Air Force was ranked as high as #4 nationally before a season-upsetting 28–21 loss at nemesis BYU. In the final Associated Press poll, the Falcons ranked eighth.

DeBerry's squads nailed three Western Athletic Conference championships: 1985, 1995, and 1998. The 1998 team's outstanding 12–1 record completed the first back-to-back 10-win seasons in school history, and the team finished the season ranked 10th nationally.

As you know, the Commander-in-Chief's Trophy is very meaningful to the players and all members of the service academies. Under DeBerry, Air Force dominated the series with arch rival military academies Army and Navy by winning the trophy 14 times and sharing it once in DeBerry's 21 seasons. Army and Navy were sure pleased when he retired.

Do all good things have to reach an end? DeBerry's last four Air Force squads lost their AF-Navy games and, subsequently, the CIC trophy each of his last 4 years at Air Force. He was a combined 34–8 against the Black Knights and Midshipmen and is the winningest coach in service academy history. DeBerry led the Academy to 12 bowl games, in which he had a respectable 6–6 record against the nation's best.

Although DeBerry had been portrayed as a role-model for most of his career, he came under fire for controversial racial remarks in October 2005 after a 48–10 loss to Texas Christian University (TCU). DeBerry said TCU "had a lot more Afro-American players than we did, and they ran a lot faster than we did. Afro-American kids can run very well. That doesn't mean that Caucasian kids and other descents can't run, but it's very obvious to me that they run extremely well."

Earlier that year, DeBerry had been criticized for a banner posted in the team's locker room that was interpreted by some as inappropriate religious proselytizing. Once you hit the top, you often become fair game for the naysayers.

Eventually, DeBerry figured his time was up and on December 15, 2006, he announced his retirement. He now splits his retirement time between South Carolina and Oklahoma, where he owns homes.

When Air Force followers look at history for a clue as to who was the finest coach in AFA history, they always stop at Fisher DeBerry. For most, it is a no-Brainer. For years before Troy Calhoun took over the program, even afterwards, someone would say, *Air Force Falcons,* and the response would quickly be **Fisher DeBerry**

Fisher DeBerry as you are about to see as we cover his 23 years in the head coach seat at Air Force, is far and away the best coach in Air Force history. He is by far the winningest coach in the history of Air Force football. On any AF coach list, DeBerry is at the top of the list.

To repeat, the legendary coach had the helm from 1984-2006 and he finished with a record of 169-109-1. You know that he had 12 bowl game appearances and 17 winning seasons during those 23 years. He also led the team to three WAC Championships.

That all amounts to him having the highest winning percentage of any Air Force coach (.608) and like few before him, was inducted into the College Football Hall of Fame in 2011.

1984 Air Force Falcons Coach Fisher DeBerry

The Air Force Falcons football team represented the United States Air Force Academy in the 1984 college football season playing as a Division I-A Independent. It was their thirtieth season of intercollegiate football. They were led by first-year head coach Fisher DeBerry in his first year at Air Force. Hatfield had already proven modern Air Force teams could win and this year, Fisher DeBerry kept it going,

Air Force had left its funk behind in 1982, renewed its former excellence on the field, and during Fisher DeBerry's tenure, they never looked back. The Falcons light never shined so bright.

Home games were played in Falcon Stadium in Colorado Springs, Colorado. The bad luck streak was over. Air Force finished the regular season with a 7–4 record overall and a 4–3 record in Western Athletic Conference games. The team was selected to play in the Independence Bowl, in which it defeated Virginia Tech

The season and home opener was played on September 1, 1984 against San Diego State at home in Falcon Stadium, Colorado Springs, CO. The Falcons turned in a fine effort for opening day, defeating Colorado State W (34-16). Air Force walloped Northern Colorado on Sep 8 at home in a major blowout W (75–7). On Sep 15 at Wyoming's War Memorial Stadium in Laramie, the Cowboys beat the Falcons L 20–26. At Utah on Sep 22 at Rice Stadium in Salt Lake City, UT, the Owls beat the Falcons L (17–28).

At home on Sep 29, the Air Force whooped Colorado State for the (Ram–Falcon Trophy) W (52–10). Then, on Oct 6 at home, Air Force defeated Navy W (29–22), Then, on Oct 13 at Notre Dame in Notre Dame Stadium in South Bend, IN, the Falcons beat the Fighting Irish W (21–7). On Oct 20 at home, Air Force was beaten by their nemesis BYU L (25–30).

Then on Nov 3at Army in Michie Stadium in West Point, NY, Air Force lost to the Cadets L (12–24). On Nov 10 at New Mexico in University Stadium, Albuquerque, NM, the Falcons beat the Lobos W (23–9). On Nov 17 in the regular season finale, at UTEP in the Sun Bowl, El Paso, TX, the Falcons beat the Miners W (38–12)

On Dec 31, New Years Eve, The 7-4 Falcons beat the Hokies of Virginia Tech in Independence Stadium, Shreveport, LA in the Independence Bowl, W (23–7), finishing the full season at 8-4. The writeup from Virginia's web site gives the highlights of the game
https://hokiesports.com/sports/2018/4/30/1984-independence-bowl.aspx?id=171

Independence Bowl
AIR FORCE 23, VIRGINIA TECH 7
December 15, 1984 - Shreveport, La.
Independence Stadium - Attendance: 41,100

SHREVEPORT, La. - Quarterback Bart Weiss got Air Force's wishbone attack going in the second half and led the Falcons to a 23-7 victory over Virginia Tech in the Independence Bowl.

Tech took a 7-3 lead in the first quarter on a 10-play, 72-yard drive that featured a 32-yard run by tailback Eddie Hunter. Maurice Williams, who alternated at the tailback spot with Hunter, capped the march with a 3-yard touchdown run.

The complexion of the game changed drastically midway through the second quarter when the Falcons forced and recovered a fumble at the Tech 3. Halfback Jody Simmons took a pitchout to the left and put Air Force ahead.

The Hokies missed a great chance to regain the lead before the half, and found themselves trailing 10-7, despite having 192 yards of offense and 11 first downs to Air Force's 73 yards and three first downs.

The news got worse for Tech in the second half when Weiss got the Falcons' ground attack going. Neither team scored in the third quarter, but Air Force controlled the football for all but eight plays of the quarter. The Falcons got a break in the fourth quarter when a halfback pass by Hunter was intercepted. From their own 38, the Falcons scored on a classic wishbone drive that ate up seven minutes and put them ahead 17-7 with just six minutes remaining in the game.
Tech's comeback hopes ended when a fumble at its own 30 set up another Air Force score. Weiss, who was named the game's most valuable offensive player, put the finishing touches on the Falcons' win with a 13-yard touchdown run.

Tech linebacker Vince Daniels, who was credited with 15 tackles, was named the game's most valuable defensive player. The scores of the game came as follows:

- AF (6:05 re 1st) - FG Maetos 35
- VT (1:42 re 1st) - Williams 3 run (Wade kick)
- AF (8:50 re 2nd) - Simmons 3 run (Maetos kick)
- AF (6:00 re 4th) - Brown 2 run (Maetos kick)
- AF (2:08 re 4th) - Weiss 13 run (kick failed)

1985 Air Force Falcons Coach Fisher DeBerry

There would be no more Air Force bad luck for many years. The Falcons finished the year ranked #5 with a phenomenal 12-1 record overall and a 7-1 record in the Western Athletic Conference (WAC) games. The team was selected to play in the BlueBonnet Bowl, in which it defeated the Texas Longhorns.

In 1985, the year bout which we are having discourse, the Falcons came within one victory of playing for the national championship. Why was that? This year it was the Nov 16 loss to BYU L (21-28). That pesky BYU team kept getting the upper hand on Air Force. Without BYU this particular year, Air Force would have been undefeated.

A few AFA Football Facts

FYI, as a writer, who has put together many sports books such as this, even if I had no major affinity and special knowledge for the team about which I am writing, by the time I finish, I am always a fan. For Air Force, Navy, and Army, teams of which I will have written books about, I had a major affinity even before as the saying goes, I put pencil to paper.

Most other teams have been around forever from the 1800's and so by the time I hit my birthday year when writing the book I am almost always at least half-through to completion. Not so with this book as Air Force is such a new program. The Falcons are scrappers for sure. I loved working through the Ben Martin years which were very good but tough for me also as Air Force was just getting its football identity.

When I saw Bill Parcells just one year at Air Force, I admit, I was concerned but now, like you, I realize Parcells was the gateway to Ken Hatfield who was the gateway to Ken Hatfield.

After Hatfield put in his startup time, he was phenomenal. His protégé Fisher DeBerry out-did his mentor for sure. For me, I wanted to take this pause in the action to tell you how much I love writing about Fisher DeBerry and the Air Force and both of their accomplishments.

I have written enough that I do not just love the Air Force because they defend my country so well; but because I now know enough about their scrappy football teams up until 1985 at least that are great beyond all explanations. Hopefully I have written and borrowed enough text about this all, that you, my readers feel the same.

As Americans we are lucky to have a great Army, a great Navy, a Great Marine Corps, A great Coast Guard, and most certainly a great Air Force. The fact that there are three service academies to produce smart servicemen in the defense of our country is a phenomenal plus. I have to admit though, I am enamored at how well they all play football while getting smart. My hat is off to them all and right now, it is well off my head as I recognize the newest branch with a service academy that also plays football – i.e. Air Force. My thank you to the great work in both uniforms (military and footballs) to the Air force

Academy. You have out-done yourselves. I am so glad that Fisher DeBerry got to help you get it done.

The 1985 season and home opener was played on August 31, 1985 against UTEP at home in Falcon Stadium, Colorado Springs, CO before 38.500. The Falcons turned in a fine effort for opening day, defeating the Miners W (48-6). On Sep 14 at Wyoming's War Memorial Stadium in Laramie, Wyoming, the Falcons were at peak in their victory W (49–7) before 29,134. At home, Rice showed up to play on Sep 21, but the Falcons refused to give the Owls and inch and prevailed in a blowout W (59–17) before 33,868. The #19 Falcons beat New Mexico on Sep in University Stadium, Albuquerque, New Mexico W 49–12 before 27,124.

Notre Dame had not caught on yet that the Air Force knew how to beat them, and Oct 5 was not the exception to the rule as the #15 Fighting Irish slid into the home of the #17 Air Force Falcons and expected a blowout in their favor. It did not happen either way as Notre Dame had to do a wiggle to get away from the Falcons W (21-15) all night and yet did not get the win. On Oct 12, Navy tried to win v # 13 Air Force but failed at Navy–Marine Corps Memorial Stadium • Annapolis, Maryland W (24–7) before 35,663.

On Oct 19 at Colorado State, the #10 Falcons beat the Rams at Hughes Stadium in Fort Collins, Colorado for the Ram–Falcon Trophy W (35–19) before 31,127. On Oct 26, at home, the #8 Falcons whooped Utah W (37–15) before 32,269. Then, on Nov 2 at home, San Diego State lost to #7 Air Force W (31–10) before 36,503. On Nov 9, at home, the #5 Falcons beat Army by a huge margin W (45–7) before 51,103.

Then, on Nov 16 at #16 BYU, the #4 Falcons suffered the BYU sting again at Cougar Stadium in Provo, Utah, L (21–28) before 65,393. After this, the only loss of the season, on Nov 23 at Hawaii, # 13 Air Force beat Hawaii at Aloha Stadium • Honolulu, HI W (27–20) before 50,000

In the post-season Bluebonnet Bowl on Dec 31 v Texas, the #10 Air Force Falcons marched into Rice Stadium in Houston, Texas, expecting a victory and due to grit and determination, they achieved their goal winning the bowl game W (24–16) before 42,000

Coming into the New Year's Eve Bluebonnet Bowl game at Rice Stadium in Houston Texas, with an 11-1 record (just a one-TD loss to BYU), the Air Force took on the Longhorns of Texas and proved again that Fisher DeBerry teams are for real. When the game was over, the Falcons had the victory by W (24-6) over the Longhorns and were crowned Bluebonnet Bowl Champions.

The Falcons counted on their unique wishbone offense after having amassed the most regular season victories in program history with eleven. We keep mentioning the one conference loss to rival and defending national champion BYU at Provo on November 16 which cost the Air Force a shot at the national title and an outright Western Athletic Conference (WAC) title. So close!

The Falcons were on a roll for sure with a fourth consecutive bowl appearance with the previous three having been victories. Unranked Texas tied for second in the Southwest Conference(SWC) but had lost to rival Texas A&M to end the regular season. It was their Texas' ninth straight bowl appearance and its first Bluebonnet Bowl in five years.

This game itself was the first Bluebonnet Bowl at Rice Stadium since 1967; the previous seventeen editions (1968–1984) were at the Astrodome. Nearly a dozen years earlier, Rice Stadium hosted Super Bowl VIII in January 1974). The kickoff was at 1:45 pm CST and about three hours late Air Force had the victory in hand.

1986 Air Force Falcons Coach Fisher DeBerry

Air Force finished the season with a 6–5 record overall and a 5–2 record in Western Athletic Conference games.

The 1986 season and home opener was played on August 30, 1986 against Hawaii at home in Falcon Stadium, Colorado Springs, CO. The game was played before 38.500. The Falcons turned in a fine effort for opening day, defeating the Rainbow Warriors W (24-7). The following week on Sep 6 at UTEP in the Sun Bowl, El Paso, TX, the Falcons edged out the Miners W (23–21). On Sep 20 at home, Wyoming beat the Air Force L (17–23). For the Ram-Falcon Trophy, at home, the Falcons defeated the Colorado State Cowboys on Sep 27

W (24–7). At Rice Stadium in Salt Lake City, UT on Oct 3, Air Force defeated Utah W (45–35).

On Oct 11 at home, Air Force pummeled Navy W (40-6). Then, on Oct 18, at Notre Dame Stadium in South Bend, IN, the Fighting Irish beat the Falcons L (3–31). Then at San Diego State on Oct 25 in Jack Murphy Stadium San Diego, CA, the Falcons prevailed W (22–10). Then, on Nov 8 at Army's Michie Stadium in West Point, NY, the Black Knights defeated the Falcons L (11–21). After a bye week on Nov 22, at Rice in Rice Stadium , Houston, TX, the Owls defeated the Falcons L (17–21). Then, on Dec 6 at home, the SFA nemesis BYU stepped up to defeat the Air Force L (3–23).

1987 Air Force Falcons Coach Fisher DeBerry

Air Force finished the season with a 9-4 record overall and a 6–2 record in Western Athletic Conference games. The Falcons offense scored 405 points while the defense allowed 269 points.

At season's end, the Falcons appeared in the 1987 Freedom Bowl. In the Ram–Falcon Trophy match, the Falcons beat the Colorado State Rams to win the trophy. Air Force also won the Commander-in-Chief's Trophy, emblematic of beating both Army and Navy.

The 1987 season opener was played on Sep 5, 1987 against Wyoming at War Memorial Stadium, Laramie, Wyoming before 28,071. The Falcons lost to the Cowboys L (13-27). On Sep 12 at home, the Air Force beat TCU W (21–10) before 41,000. At home on Sep 19, Air Force beat San Diego State W (49–7) in a blowout before 35,035. At Colorado State on Sep 26 in Hughes Stadium, Fort Collins, Colorado (Battle for the Ram–Falcon Trophy), the Air Force prevailed W (27–19) before 23,137. Then, on Oct 3 at home, Air Force beat UtahW (48–27) before 35,108

At Navy on Oct 10, in Navy–Marine Corps Memorial Stadium, Annapolis, Maryland, the Falcons beat the Midshipmen W (23–13) for the first half of the Commander-In-Chief's Trophy before 35,622. On Oct 17 at home, #11 Notre Dame beat Air Force L (14–35) before 51,112. On Oct 24, at home, Air Force beat UTEP W (35–7) before 36,922. On Oct 31 BYU beat Air Force again at Cougar Stadium Provo, Utah, L (13–24) before 65,384. On Nov 7, Air Force won the

Commander-In-Chief's Trophy when they beat Army at home W (27–10) before 49,183.

On Nov 14 at New Mexico's University Stadium in Albuquerque, New Mexico, the Falcons shellacked the Lobos W (73–26) in a blowout before 15,309. On Nov 21 at Hawaii's Aloha Stadium, Honolulu, HI, the Falcons edged out the Rainbow Warriors W (34–31) before 43,340

After having won four straight bowl games, the Air Force lost on December 30, 1987 to Arizona State in Anaheim Stadium, Anaheim, California in the Freedom Bowl L (28–33) before 33,261.

Freedom Bowl Highlights

Air Force played tough, but it was not enough as Daniel Ford, Arizona State's junior quarterback, threw for 272 yards, including a 61-yard touchdown to Aaron Cox that capped a 24-point second quarter, enabling the Sun Devils to beat Air Force, 33-28, in the Freedom Bowl.

Coach John Cooper's Sun Devils finished 7-4-1. Cooper will be coaching at Ohio State next season. Air Force finished at 9-4. Ford completed 16 of 30 attempts in amassing the most passing yardage in his college career. Channing Williams and Darryl Harris scored on 2-yard runs for Arizona State in the second quarter, and Kirk Wendorf scored on a 20-yard run in the fourth quarter.

Arizona State converted two turnovers by Steve Letnich, the Air Force quarterback, into 10 points in the second quarter on the way to their 24-14 halftime lead.

The Sun Devils bumped up the lead to 33-14 in the second half despite having two scores called back because of penalties. Arizona State, which turned the ball over three times in the third quarter, got out of the period with a 20-yard field goal by Alan Zendejas.

Zendejas also missed two kicks and connected from 36 yards in the second quarter. The Falcons played without the services of their top quarterback, Dee Dowis, who broke his hand in the regular-season finale against Hawaii. Dowis had established a National Collegiate

Athletic Association rushing record for quarterbacks by gaining 1,315 yards.

The Arizona State defense was led by Shawn Patterson, a tackle. They held the Air Force's wishbone offense to 276 yards. Letnich, who replaced Dowis as the starter, gained 90 yards in 16 carries.

The Falcons' Steven Senn caught scoring passes of 10 and 18 yards from a reserve quarterback, Lance McDowell, in the last three minutes as Air Force reduced the margin but could not squeeze out a victory.

1988 Air Force Falcons Coach Fisher DeBerry

The 1988 season opener was played on September 3, 1988 against Colorado State at Sonny Lubick Field at Hughes Stadium , Fort Collins, Colorado. The Falcons defeated the Rams W (29-23). On Sep 11, San Diego State defeated Air Force at Jack Murphy Stadium in San Diego L (36–39). On Sep 17, Air Force walloped Northwestern at home W (62–27) before 42,612. Wyoming edged out Air Force on Sep 24 at home L (45–48). On Oct 8, the Falcons beat the Midshipmen at home W (33–24). At Utah on Oct 15 in Rice Stadium, Salt Lake City, Air Force prevailed W (56–49).

Then, on Oct 22 at Notre Dame in Notre Dame Stadium, Notre Dame, Indiana, the Fighting Irish beat the Falcons L (13–41) On Nov 5, at Army's Michie Stadium, West Point, New York, the Black Knights beat the Falcons L (15–28). At home on Nov 12, BYU beat Air Force again L (31–49). Then, on Nov 19 at UTEP in Sun Bowl Stadium, El Paso, Texas, the Miners beat the Falcons L (24–31). In the season finale, on Nov 26 at Hawaii's Aloha Stadium Honolulu, HI The Rainbow Warriors beat the Falcons L (14–19).

1989 Air Force Falcons Coach Fisher DeBerry

The 1989 season and home opener was played on September 2, 1989 against San Diego State. The Falcons defeated the Aztecs in a shootout W (52-36). At home, on Sep 10, Air Force shellacked Wyoming W (45-7) before 44,098. At Northwestern on Sep 16 at Dyche Stadium in Evanston, Illinois, the Air Force won its third in a row. W (48-31) before 27,334. At home on Sep 23, the Air Force defeated UTEP, W (43-26) before 43,898. At Colorado State in the battle for the Ram-Falcon Trophy, on Sep 30 in Hughes Stadium Fort Collins, Colorado, #24 Air Force defeated the RAMS, W (46-21) before 30,955

At Navy on Oct 7 in Navy–Marine Corps Memorial Stadium, Annapolis, Maryland, the Falcons beat the Midshipmen W (35-7) before 35,632. Playing against #1 ranked Notre Dame at home on Oct 14at home, the #17 Falcons put up a good battle then lost to the Fighting Irish L (27-41) before 53,533. On Oct 21 at TCU, the #19 Falcons lost to the Horned Frogs in Amon G. Carter Stadium , Fort Worth, Texas L (9-27) before 23,593

Air Force grabbed the Commander-in-Chief's Trophy and Army, when the Falcons beat the Black Knights on Nov 4 at home in Falcon Stadium W (29-3) before 52,226. #21 BYU kept their "best nemesis" status on Nov 11 in Cougar Stadium Provo, Utah L (35-44) before 66,089. On Nov 25 at Utah in Rice Stadium, Salt Lake City, Utah, the Air Force prevailed, W (42-38) before 20,119. After a two-week break at Hawaii, on Dec 9, in Aloha Stadium Honolulu, HI, the teams played to a tie T (35-35) before 37,604

The Liberty Bowl committee invited Air Force to play Mississippi on December 28, 1989 in Liberty Bowl Memorial Stadium Memphis, Tennessee. The Rebels defeated the Falcons L 29-42 before 60,128.

Liberty Bowl Highlights Dec 28, 1989

Air Force had a string broken in the prior year's bowl game and they lost again this time in 1989 in the Liberty Bowl, This game was played between the Ole Miss Rebels (42) and the Air Force Falcons (29).

The Rebels had a great year, finishing tied for 4th in the Southeastern Conference while the Falcons finished 2nd in the Western Athletic Conference. This was the first year in which the winner of the Commander in Chief's Trophy (Air Force) received an automatic bid to the Liberty Bowl. Air Force was pleased to accept.

The two teams had played before in 1983. Chucky Mullins, an Ole Miss favorite, who had been paralyzed in a game just two months prior, visited the Ole Miss locker room prior to the game in his first visit outside the hospital since before his injury.

It was a well-played game with the first quarter bringing Ole Miss a score with Hines' 32 pass from Darnell. Hogue got the PAT with 3:53 remaining. Then Air Force got a Wood 37 FG with 11:16 remaining. Ole Miss's Baldwin scored on a 23 run with a Hogue PAT, and there was 9:18 remaining. Air Force then had a Dowis 2 yd run; but a pass failed with 3:19 remaining

Despite all the hard work, the Falcons lost the game L (29-42)

1990 Air Force Falcons Coach Fisher DeBerry

The 1990 season and home opener was played on September 1, 1990 against Colorado State. The Rams defeated the Falcons in a close match W (33-35). This win gave the Rams this year's (Ram–Falcon Trophy). On Sep 8 at home, the Air Force beat Hawaii W (27–3). Then, at home again on Sep 15 The Air Force beat Citadel W (10-7). On Sep 22, at Wyoming in War Memorial Stadium Laramie, WY, the Cowboys beat the Falcons L (12–24). On Sep 29 at San Diego State in Jack Murphy Stadium, San Diego, CA, the Aztecs beat the Falcons L 18–48. On Oct 6 at home, Air Force beat Navy W (24–7)

On Oct 13, at Notre Dame, the Fighting Irish thumped the Air Force in a blowout in Notre Dame Stadium , Notre Dame, IN L (27–57). On Oct 27 Air Force walloped Utah at home W (52–21). On Nov 3, BYU, a continual nemesis to the Falcons squashed Air Force at home L (7–54). On Nov 10, Air Force won the Commander-in-Chief's Trophy as the Falcons beat the Army Black Knights at Michie Stadium, West Point, NY W (15–3). Air Force then beat UTEP on Nov 27 at the Sun Bowl in El Paso, TX W (14–13) to wrap up the regular season.

As the winner of the Commander-in-Chief's Trophy, Air Force was invited again to the Liberty Bowl. On December 27, 1990 v Ohio State. The game was played in Liberty Bowl Memorial Stadium in Memphis, TN. The Air Force prevailed W (23–11).

Highlights of the 1990 Liberty Bowl

Fisher DeBerry's 1990 Falcons triumphed over "THE" Ohio State in the 1990 Liberty Bowl. It was great for the Falcons but the loss was especially hurtful to Ohio State as it came on the heels of Coach John Cooper's third straight loss to Michigan as Ohio State's head coach. It changed their season. If Ohio State had won that game, Ohio State would have gone to the Rose Bowl. Instead, Ohio State was sent to Memphis to play against an Air Force team that barely qualified for bowl eligibility. In retrospect, I would think the Buckeyes wished they had spent a bit more time thinking about the game rather than their "humiliation."

Despite outsizing and outweighing the Air Force Defense, the Buckeyes simply could not get the run going. Their famed back Robert Smith, for example, was held to just 62 rushing yards and one touchdown. OSU QB Greg Frey was terrible, throwing for just 10 of 27 for 110 yards. He also threw an interception before being taken out and replaced by Kent Graham late in the game.

OSU had a 5-0 lead in the first due to recovering a muffed punt in the end zone for a safety and later gaining a field goal. But Perez gave the Air Force the lead with 3:42 in the half on a touchdown sneak, entering halftime with a 6-5 lead. He added another touchdown run to make it 13-5 in the third quarter.

Ohio State narrowed the Falcon lead to 13-11 and so they went for two to tie. But Graham's pass was too high thus keeping the difference at 2. The Falcons kept at it by adding a field goal after a bad punt, making it 16-11. While driving to try to take the lead, Air Force intercepted Frey's and Carlton McDonald returned it 40 yards. This was McDonald's second of the day).

This assured the win for Air Force. Rob Perez only threw 1 for 3 passes (a Liberty Bowl record for least amount of pass completions) for 11 yards and an interception. He also rushed for 93 yards and 2 touchdowns for Fisher DeBerry's well-oiled Air Force squad.

1991 Air Force Falcons Coach Fisher DeBerry

The Falcons had a great year and came very close to playing for the national championship.

The 1991 season and home opener was played on Aug 31, 1991 against Weber State. The Falcons defeated the Wildcats W (48-31) before 41,294. At Colorado State, on Sep 7, in Hughes Stadium Fort Collins, Colorado for the Ram–Falcon Trophy, the Falcons prevailed W (31–26) before 31,977. At Utah on Sep 14 in Rice Stadium Salt Lake City, the Falcons beat the Utes W (24–21) before 28,619. Then, on Sep 21 at home, Air Force nosed out San Diego State W (21–20) before 43,011. On Sep 28 at BYU, in Cougar Stadium, Provo, Utah, the Cougars beat the Falcons L (7–21) before 65,899.

On Oct 5 at home, the Falcons beat the Wyoming Cowboys W (51–28) before 40,227. At Navy on Oct 12 in Navy–Marine Corps Memorial Stadium • Annapolis, Maryland for the Commander-in-Chief's Trophy' Air Force dominated and won big W (46–6) before 35,640. At home, on Oct 19, Notre Dame beat Air Force L (15–28) before 52,024. At home on Oct 26, Air Force beat UTEP W (20–13) before 38,975.

On Nov 2 at New Mexico's University Stadium in Albuquerque, New Mexico, the Lobos defeated the Falcons L (32–34) before 10,793. On Nov 9, Air Force shut out Army at home and won the Commander-in-Chief's Trophy w (25-0) before 49,203. At Hawaii on Nov 23 in Aloha Stadium, Honolulu, HI for the Kuter Trophy, the Falcons defeated the Rainbow Warriors W (24–20) before 36,884.

Having won the Commander-in-Chief's Trophy, the Falcons were invited to the Liberty Bowl on December 29 vs. Mississippi State. The game was played in Liberty Bowl Stadium, Memphis, Tennessee where the Falcons defeated the Volunteers W 38-15 before 61,497

1991 Liberty Bowl Highlights

Fullback Jason Jones and Rob Perez each with one-yard scoring runs gave the Falcons a 14-0 first quarter lead. Perez's TD came just six plays after the kickoff returner fumbled the ball back to the Falcons.

The score shot up to 21-0 when Shannon Yates recovered a fumble and ran 35 yards for a touchdown. Sleepy Robinson threw a touchdown pass to Trenell Edwards to culminate a 76-yard drive with thirty-five seconds left in the half.

The Falcons hit a lull and scored only three points in the third quarter, though they had possession of the ball for 13:12. Scott Hufford scored on a 31-yard touchdown run on the 2nd play of the fourth quarter. Michael Davis then ran for a touchdown to make it 31-15 with 7:23 remaining, but the Falcons would not be beaten, Rob Perez ran for a whopping 318 yards while only attempting two passes in the entire game. Air Force outgained the Bulldogs in time of possession by 37:34 to 22:26.

1992 Air Force Falcons Coach Fisher DeBerry

The 1992 season and home opener was played on Sep 5, 1992 against Rice in Falcon Stadium • Colorado Springs, CO. The Falcons defeated the Owls W (30-21). On Sep 12, at home, Hawaii beat the Falcons in a close match L (3-6). At Wyoming on Sep 19 in War Memorial Stadium Laramie, WY, the Falcons beat the Cowboys W (42–28). Then, on Sep 26, at home, Air Force nosed out New Mexico W (33–32). On Oct 3, Air Force defeated UTEP in Sun Bowl Stadium El Paso, TX, W (28–22). Then, on Oct 10 at home, Air Force edged out Navy for the first game of this year's Commander-in-Chief's Trophy competition W (18–16).

At home on Oct 17, for the Ram-Falcon Trophy, Colorado State defeated Air force L 28–32. At San Diego State's Jack Murphy Stadium in San Diego, CA, on Oct 24, Air Force defeated the Aztecs W (20–17). At home again on Oct 31, Utah defeated Air Force L (13–20). On Nov 7, in a close match, Air Force won the Commander-in-Chief's Trophy by defeating Army in Michie Stadium West Point, NY W 7–3. On Nov 14, perennial nemesis BYU beat Air Force at home L (7–28) to close out the regular season.

On Dec 31, Air Force was shut out by Ole Miss in the Liberty Bowl, played in Liberty Bowl Memorial Stadium Memphis, TN L (0–13)

Liberty Bowl Game Highlights

Ole Miss's Dou Innocent started things off with a TD to give the Rebels a 7-0 lead over Air Force's Falcons with 2:42 left in the first quarter. He completed his day with 65 yards on 17 carries. Brian Lee kicked two field goals from 24 and 29 yards making the final game score 13-0 as Air Force was held to a minimal offensive production (185 yards of total offense). Russ Shows completed 9-of-19 for 163 yards. Cassius Ware had 10 tackles and 2 sacks, in a game MVP effort.

1993 Air Force Falcons Coach Fisher DeBerry

The 1993 season and home opener was played on September 4, 1993 against Indiana State in Falcon Stadium Colorado Springs, CO. The Falcons pounded the Sycamores in a blowout W (63-21). On Sep 11 at Colorado State in Hughes Stadium Fort Collins, Colorado (Ram–Falcon Trophy), in a low-scoring match, the Rams beat the Falcons L (5–8). On Sep 18 at home, San Diego State beat Air Force L (31–38).

Then, at BYU on Sep 25 in Cougar Stadium, Provo, Utah, the Cougars beat the Falcons L (3–30). On Oct 2 at home, Wyoming beat Air Force L (18–31). On Oct 9, at Navy's Navy–Marine Corps Memorial Stadium in Annapolis, Maryland, the Midshipmen beat the Falcons L 24–28 On Oct 16 at Fresno State in Bulldog Stadium Fresno, California, the Bulldogs beat the Falcons L (20–33). On Oct 23, at home, Air Force shutout The Citadel W (35–0)

At home on Oct 30, Air Force beat UTEP W (31–10). On Nov 6 at home, Air Force defeated Army in the Commander-in-Chief's Trophy battle. W (25–6). Since AFA won the prior year and since Army beat Navy, the three-way tie resulted in Air Force retaining the Trophy. On Nov 13 at Utah in Rice Stadium Salt Lake City, the Owls beat the Falcons L (24–41). At Hawaii's Aloha Stadium in Honolulu, HI, on Nov 20, the Rainbow Warriors beat the Falcons L (17-45)

1994 Air Force Falcons Coach Fisher DeBerry

The 1994 season and home opener was played on September 3, 1994 against Colorado State in Falcon Stadium • Colorado Springs, CO. The Falcons lost to the Rams for the Ram-Falcon Trophy L (21-34). At home on Sep 10, BYU beat the Air Force for the twelfth year in a row L (21-45).

At home again on Sep 17 Northwestern beat the Air Force L (10–14). On Sep 24, Air Force pounded UTEP in the Alamo dome San Antonio, TX in a blowout W (47–7) After three losses in a row, it was good to see the AF offense engaged.

On Oct 1at San Diego State's Jack Murphy Stadium • San Diego, CA, the Falcons nosed out the Aztecs. At home on Oct 8, Air Force defeated Navy on their way to winning the Commander-in-Chief's Trophy W (43–21). At home v Fresno State, on Oct 22, the Falcons prevailed W (42–7). Then, on Oct 29 at Wyoming in War Memorial Stadium Laramie, WY, the Falcons beat the Cowboys W (34–17).

On Nov 5, Air Force beat Army by a hair at Michie Stadium West Point, NY W (10–6) earning the Commander-in-Chief's Trophy for the Falcons. On Nov 12, at home, Air Force beat Utah W (40–33). Then, on Nov 19 at Notre Dame in Notre Dame Stadium Notre Dame, IN, in a tough match, the Fighting Irish defeated the Falcons L (30–42). In the Season finale, on Dec 3 at Hawaii in Aloha Stadium • Honolulu, HI, the Air Force beat the Rainbow Warriors W (37–24)

1995 Air Force Falcons Coach Fisher DeBerry

The 1995 season and home opener was played on September 2, 1995 against BYU in Falcon Stadium • Colorado Springs, CO. The Falcons beat the Cougars after twelve years of losses W (38-12). It took Fisher DeBerry twelve years to beat BYU. From this point on there would be a mix of wins and losses for BYU and the Falcons. The long win drought with Brigham Young University for the Air Force, was finally over. They were still a nemesis, but their probability of winning had been decreased substantially.

At home on Sep 9, Air Force defeated Wyoming W 34–10. Then, on Sep 16, at home, an always tough Colorado State squad beat the then ranked #21 Air Force squad and won the Ram–Falcon Trophy L (20–27). At Northwestern on Sep 23 in Dyche Stadium Evanston, IL, the Falcons were beaten by the Wildcats L (6–30). On Sep 30 at New Mexico in University Stadium Albuquerque, NM, the Falcons edged out the Lobos W 27–24. At home on Oct 7, Air Force defeated UTEP W (56–43). Then on Oct 14 at Navy's Navy–Marine Corps Memorial Stadium Annapolis, MD for the first half of the

Commander-in-Chief's Trophy, the Falcons beat the Midshipmen W (30–20).

On Oct 21 at Utah in Rice Stadium Salt Lake City, Utah, the Utes outgunned the Air Force in a tough match L (21–22). Then, at Fresno State on Oct 28 in a game played at Bulldog Stadium Fresno, CA, Air Force prevailed W (31–20). For the full capture of the Commander-in-Chief's Trophy, Air Force had already beaten Navy and on Nov 11, Army fell to the AFA Juggernaut at home in Falcon Stadium W (38-20).

Always struggling against Notre Dame, 1005 would be no different as on Nov 18 at home, Notre Dame defeated the Air Force at Falcon Stadium L (14–44). In the last game of the regular season, I can't believe there was one officer or airman who objected to a trip on Nov 25 to play Hawaii at Aloha Stadium Honolulu, HI. The second-best part of the trip for Airforce (after having a wonderful experience in the islands) was their great victory over the long-time rival Rainbow Warriors W (45–28).

After such a great regular season, Air Force played in the Copper Bowl on December 27 vs. Texas Tech in Arizona Stadium Tucson, AZ. The Copper Bowl was a shootout so both the offensive and defensive squads in this match felt OK but only Texas Tech actually felt good as the won the game L 41–55)

Copper Bowl Highlights

The Air Force was invited to the 1995 Copper Bowl played on December 27, 1995, at Arizona Stadium in Tucson, Arizona. Most Americans have never heard of the Copper Bowl; but it takes a while. It turns out that it was just the seventh edition of the annual Copper Bowl—now known by fans as the Cactus Bowl. This game featured the Texas Tech Red Raiders, and the Air Force Falcons.

Both teams were ready to take away the bowl trophy. This year, the Red Raiders were 1-2 against ranked opponents, having lost to #4 Penn State and #13 Texas but they did beat #8 Texas A&M.

The Red Raiders finished tied for 2nd in the Southwest Conference with Texas A&M and Baylor. It was their third bowl game in two seasons. Air Force, which had gotten over its phobia about beating BYU, finished as co-champion of the Western Athletic Conference in a rare four-way tie, with Colorado State, BYU, and Utah.

Air Force had beaten BYU to begin the season, but they lost to Colorado State and Utah. However, Fisher DeBerry's Falcons were the only one of the four to be invited to a bowl game, their 7th in 10 seasons.

Air Force held their ground for the most part in the game but gave up just enough to lose the shootout contest L (41-55).

Chapter 10 Coach Fisher DeBerry 1996-2006

DeBerry   Coach # 6

Year	Coach	Record	Conf	Record
1996	Fisher DeBerry	6–5	WAC	5–3
1997	Fisher DeBerry	10–3	WAC	6–2
1998	Fisher DeBerry	12–1	WAC	7–1
1999	Fisher DeBerry	6–5	MWC	2–5
2000	Fisher DeBerry	9–3	MWC	5–2
2001	Fisher DeBerry	6–6	MWC	3–4
2002	Fisher DeBerry	8–5	MWC	4–3
2003	Fisher DeBerry	7–5	MWC	3–4
2004	Fisher DeBerry	5–6	MWC	3–4
2005	Fisher DeBerry	4–7	MWC	3–5
2006	Fisher DeBerry	4–8	MWC	3–4

As you have surely deduced by now, coaches Ben Martin and Fisher DeBerry put in twenty-+ years at the helm for Air Force. And so, my knowing that readers of great books such as this, Ahem, are known to not want to read forever and ever to get finished one single chapter so they can get on to the next. So for these legendary coaches, I chose to split the chapters about down the middle and give the reader a nice break in-between.

The good news for all readers is that we still have eleven more Fisher DeBerry chapters. I suspect that you like reading about this phenomenal coach as I like writing about him. He makes me wish I was one of the chosen to be on his college football squad while his squads were all trying to become Air Force Pilots.

In 1969, by the way, as I prepared for graduation at King's College in Wilkes-Barre PA, I tried my best to get in the Air Force, along with my buddy, Bucko Grimes. Since the targets I identified in the spotting exercises for pilot and navigator positions all looked to me like fingerprints in FBI files, I did not think I would be able to guess any of the questions correctly. I was right.

I qualified for every Officer position other than Pilot and Navigator. If you had seen what I saw in the site testing, you would not have waned me on your plane in any official capacity.

At the time in 1969, the Air Force told me I qualified for every other position than Pilot and Navigator and they kindly asked me to pick three. If, of the three positions, there were no openings, they would get back to me and give me another round of MOS choices. Apparently AFA graduates had taken the positions for which I would qualify. Nobody told me that. I just figured.

In the meantime, as a twenty-one year old fresh college graduate, I was called in for my Draft-Board physical. Knowing I was an Air Force potential candidate was not an excuse to avoid the Draft, and that was not what I was looking for anyway. Since I had moved for work to IBM in Utica, NY, I requested my physical be moved to my new residence in Utica, NY. I had not heard about my second three selections from the Air Force. I wanted to join, not be drafted.

A few friends suggested that I go to the Utica National Guard as Sergeant Frost, the Commander liked College Graduates. When the Draft physical was imminent, made the call and Sergeant Frost and I had a nice interview and he told me about the Utica National Guard. He set up a physical for me and I passed before my Draft physical. I took my oath shortly and by the end of the year I was in Basic Training.

Everybody tells me how fortunate I am but to this day, I know my first goal was to be in the Air Force. When my buddy Bucko Grimes writes his book some-day about something for sure, I suspect he'll say something pretty close to what I said. Neither of us wanted to be drafted but we wanted to serve. He was the guy that suggested I go for an Air Force Career. Now you know the rest of the story.

In 1996, I was beginning my second year at King's College in Wilkes-Barre, PA. What a great school! While many in the US were protesting the Vietnam War, my peers at Kings engaged a pro-War march to Public Square in Wilkes-Barre, PA. Call us bumpkins or whatever you want. For me, avoiding the call to serve America was not in the cards, and my college felt the same.

This chapter begins in 1996, which happened to be my sophomore year in college. Ten years later, this great coach would retire from football. But, he had eleven good years in front of him. for real.

It is no secret for anybody that Fisher DeBerry retired in December 2006 after his last season. So, before we go on to see the next eleven years of his career, I thought I would show you what the press was writing about him eleven years later in 2006, while this great coach was saying good-bys. It will help us all to appreciate the details in the next eleven sections as we recount the seasons leading up to his retirement.

Enjoy!

Dec. 15, 2006
Fisher DeBerry announces retirement as head coach at Air Force

https://goairforcefalcons.com/news/2006/12/15/Fisher_DeBerry_announces_retirement_as_head_coach_at_Air_Force.aspx

U.S. AIR FORCE ACADEMY, Colo. - Air Force head football coach Fisher DeBerry announced his retirement today, ending over a quarter-century at the Air Force Academy.

DeBerry just completed his 23rd season as the head football coach and 27th overall at Air Force. DeBerry has guided the Falcons to 17 winning seasons since taking over in 1984. He's guided the Academy to three conference championships. Air Force won the Western Athletic Conference title in 1985 and again in 1995. In 1998, DeBerry guided the team to its first out-right title and a championship game win over its long-time nemesis Brigham Young. His 1998 team matched the school record with a 12-1 season while earning him his third coach of the year award.

The Cheraw, S.C., native has done it all at Air Force. He is the winningest coach in school history with a 169-107-1 mark. He stands second in Mountain West Conference history in career wins with 100, trailing only close friend and former BYU coach LaVell Edwards. He has also beaten Notre Dame three times, including a 20-17 overtime thriller against the eighth-ranked Irish in South Bend in 1996.

DeBerry has dominated service academy football. In 1999, DeBerry became the winningest coach in service academy football history when AFA knocked off Washington in Seattle. He is an amazing 35-11 against Army and Navy in his career and has led the Academy to 14 of its 16 Commander-in-Chief's trophy titles.

DeBerry is a 1960 graduate of Wofford College in Spartanburg, S.C., where he lettered in football and baseball. After six years of coaching and teaching in the South Carolina high school ranks, DeBerry returned to Wofford, where he stayed two years as an assistant when the school won 21 consecutive games and was ranked No. 1 nationally. It was during a nine-year stop at Appalachian State in Boone, N.C., where his work with the option offense began to blossom. Appalachian State ranked in the top 10 nationally three times (1975, `78, `79) in rushing, total offense or scoring offense under DeBerry.

Former Air Force head coach Ken Hatfield hired DeBerry in 1980 as the quarterbacks coach at Air Force. DeBerry was promoted to offensive coordinator in 1981. When Hatfield left Air Force after the 1983 season, DeBerry became the school's sixth head coach (counting 1955 when AFA played only Freshman teams.)

DeBerry and his wife, LuAnn, are active in community affairs. The coach gives motivational speeches and has worked tirelessly with several local and national charities. The couple started the Fisher DeBerry Foundation recently which is an organization to benefit single-parent families in Colorado Springs. DeBerry is also active with the Fellowship of Christian Athletes and in 2001 authored a book "For God and Country" of which the proceeds go to the FCA.

The coach has received several regional and national awards for his work off the field. He has been honored with the State Farm Coach of Distinction Award for his efforts on and off the field in 2001. This past summer, DeBerry was selected for induction into the Colorado Springs Sports Hall of Fame. He is also a member of the South Carolina Sports Hall of Fame.

Retirement STATEMENT FROM Fisher DeBerry

There comes a time in every man's life when you have to look at the big picture and decide what's the best thing for your family. After 27 exciting and wonderful years here at the Academy and a total of 44 years of coaching, I am announcing my retirement from active coaching.

Coaching is the best job a guy could have, but it is a very demanding and time-consuming job. My kids and grandkids have moved to Oklahoma. It is time for Lu Ann and me to spend some quality time together and be with them. We passionately love the Academy and consider it an honor and a privilege to have had the opportunity to serve here and carry the title "Coach."

We respect the military so much and the mission of the Academy and I have felt football is one of the most important leadership training opportunities here. We have been blessed and privileged to have had the opportunity to coach the finest young people in America and work daily with the best coaches in NCAA football. Nobody in life does anything by themselves [The only thing you can do alone in life—is fail]. and any success we have enjoyed is the direct result of a tremendous commitment on the part of so many; the players, coaches, secretary, support staff and administration.

Therefore, this is the hardest decision I have ever made in my life. I love my players and my coaches. I will always be grateful to former Superintendent Gen. Skip Scott and former Athletic Director John Clune for their confidence and the opportunity they gave me 23 years ago to live my dream.

It's been a good ride and I thank from the bottom of my heart all my players and my fellow coaches over my tenure for their commitment to excellence and high expectations. I especially want to thank the best secretary in NCAA football for 25 years of loyal and faithful service to the football program.

In conclusion, I want to thank my loving wife of 41 years, Lu Ann, for her understanding loving support and commitment and for putting up with late suppers. Thank you, Baby, for your love and support. Also, I thank my two children, Joe and Michelle, for their support during this ride. Without their love, I wouldn't be standing here today. No question, Lu Ann has been the Head Coach and we have been a good team.

Finally, I want to thank my Master Coach for leading us to Colorado 26 years ago. I pray we have made a difference in the lives of the ones who have been entrusted to us and I hope we have honored Him in all we have tried to do. We love Colorado and especially Colorado Springs and the wonderful friends we have made. I hope Lu Ann and I can continue to be of service to others in this community.

As I have always said to others departing the program, `Once a Falcon, Always a Falcon.' My heart and prayers will always be with the Fighting Falcons. Thanks to all for the privilege and opportunity to have been able to serve the finest educational institution in the country and the finest kids in the world. Thanks to this community and Denver, some of the greatest football fans in the nation, for your support over the years. When I came to the Academy, a good crowd was between 15, 000 and 18,000. Today we have averaged well over 40,000 during my career here.

To you, the press, I have enjoyed working with you and proud to call you friends. Thanks for the positive things you write about our athletes and the total athletic program here at the Academy.

Lu Ann and I are so humbled, honored and thankful for the opportunity and are excited now to see what God's plan is for our future. Thank you and have a great day.

STATEMENT FROM DR. HANS MUEH, USAFA ATHLETIC DIRECTOR

"Thank you all for coming. It has been a difficult week for everyone involved because of the announcement that coach is going to make. Before I bring Fisher up, I want to say a few words about what he has meant to the Academy. Fisher DeBerry has made countless contributions over the 25 years that he has been here...both on and off the field. He has been a solid role model for all of our core values - integrity, service and excellence - in all he has done for us. His legacy is certainly intact."

Question and Answer Session with Dr. Mueh

Q: Was there any pressure put on Fisher to make any changes? Is that what made him come to this decision?

A: We had our normal, end-of-season discussion. We met a couple of times, talked about it and bounced ideas back and forth. Ultimately, Fisher just decided that it was time. Coming from the military, you always know when it's time to put your papers in to retire. And I think that in Fisher's case, he just decided that it was time.

Q: Would he have been able to return keeping the same staff as he had this year?

A: Possibly...although I left that decision (to him). We talked and when he came back and said that he was going to leave...any discussion about future plans ceased. At that point, it was sort of moot.

Q: What about the remainder of his contract? Does it just end now or is there some role that he could fill in the future to fulfill his contract?

A: Fisher will always have a role at the Academy. I would never deny him that. He will always be, like he said, a Falcon. Once a Falcon, always a Falcon. In terms of any specific work that he would do for us...that hasn't been defined yet. Let me defer (salary questions) until later. This is Fisher's moment and I don't need to get into those details.

Q: What about his assistants? What is their status?

A: I think Fisher called all of them last night to let them know the situation. I would assume after we identify a new head coach...that many of Fisher's staff will be strongly considered for roles in the next staff. But at this point, I can't comment on specifics.

Q: After the TCU game you said that you really didn't have a short list ready for coaching candidates. Do you have one now?

A: Yes, my short list now is every coach in the NCAA. It's an interesting question. In my experience, when my basketball coach left on short notice, my experience was that I got inundated with requests because people out there in America understand what Fisher has created here at the Air Force Academy. A legacy of winning, a legacy of football prominence. I anticipate that we will get the same type of calls once this hits the street. My mind is wide open when it comes to future coaches.

Q: Do you have an ideal timetable for when you would like to have someone in mind?

A: Yeah, like by tomorrow. No, really though, as soon as possible. And the only reason I say that is because we are in the recruiting season. It is vital that all of those contacts that our current assistants have made continue to be contacts and followed up and so on. The quicker that I can identify a new coach and a staff for the future, the better off this program will be. In my perfect world, I would love to have this done before the holidays, yes. Whether or not I can pull that off, I don't know.

Q: Will any of the current assistants be considered seriously for head coach?

A: We will interview anyone who is interested. Yes, absolutely.

Q: Would you look at someone with an Academy background specifically, or does that not matter?

A: I think that helps, but I don't think that it is an absolute requirement.

AIR FORCE PLAYER QUOTES

Shaun Carney, Quarterback (Senior in 2007) The meeting with coach was pretty emotional this morning. He really poured his heart out to us. We really weren't surprised, but we really didn't expect it either.

I would like to see the qualities in our new that Coach DeBerry had. When it comes to how much we learned from him as people off the field. He always taught us to be a great father and great husband and a man of great character. Those are qualities that we take from him. We would always like to see a coach that brings some intensity to the table and Coach De Berry always did that. I would like to see our new coach emulate Coach DeBerry in a lot of ways.

I think he was ready to retire. He talked about how his family played an integral part of his decision and how he wanted to spend more time with his grandchildren. I really think that his decision was more about his family than about him.

Any losing season leaves a sour taste in our mouths. My class hasn't had a winning season yet and that never happened under Coach DeBerry. We want to get the new coach off to a great start.

You can't point fingers at the coaches or at the players. As players we have to work harder and get better and grow as players and as people and get ready for next season.

I think we have some great athletes on the offensive side of the ball and have a lot of experience. I think we can adapt to any new coach or new system. As a quarterback, I love to throw the ball, but more importantly I like to win football games and it isn't something that I've done here. In my last season, I'd like to be remembered as someone that won games and went to a bowl game.

Drew Fowler, Linebacker (Senior in 2007) It was pretty shocking. I didn't ever think that while I was here (coach DeBerry would retire). It's just one of those things.

Whoever comes in, I hope they understand the kind of people we have here and the kind of program we run here. We need to keep going from where Coach DeBerry has started us. He's obviously had great intentions for us, and we need to build on that

I hope we don't look at next year as a rebuilding year. I really don't want my senior year to be thought of that way. I think we have enough tools on this team to be competitive just like we are every year. We just need to figure out a way to win close games, that's what it boils down to.

I'll miss Coach DeBerry's little comments on everyday life things. There is probably no one in this world that cares more about us than Coach DeBerry. That is something hard to find now days. Everyone is so caught up in winning that sometimes they forget about their players. With Coach, it was always the team before anything.

He is a great role model. Words can't explain what it means to the players when a head football coach shows emotion like today. Coach DeBerry and Coach (Richard) Bell are the people that brought me here and gave me a chance to play when no one else thought I could do it at the D-I level. I give them thanks for that. They opened doors for me that I could have never opened myself.

Bobby Giannini, Safety (Senior in 2007) When he announced that he was retiring, I think we all had that vibe. But we support him in whatever he does--if he would have stayed or that he has retired. I don't think it was a surprise. We can always say that we played for a Hall of Fame class coach. His message was a very somber one this morning. He just looked sad.

It's not going to be a rebuilding year because we have so many seniors coming back. I'm not worried about that.

Having a new coach can be good or can be bad, but we'll just see how it goes. We were certainly sad to see Coach DeBerry go, but we are excited to get things going for next year.
Dr. Mueh, our AD, told us that he promised the basketball team that after their coach left that he would bring in a coach that would bring them more success than we have had before, and he promised us the same thing.

Ryan Williams, Fullback (Senior in 2007) My initial reaction was that a decision he had to make. He had to think about what was best for his family and I stand by that. You can't argue with that.

It is sad to see him go. He recruited me with Coach Petersen. It will be a little different to have a different coach. I think it would be nice for our new coach to have a lot of energy and pick us up.

On a potential new offense: It's our job to play and not coach so whatever the new coach throws out there for us, we have to do. This decision is not going to change anything the way I work in the off-season. We'll just go out and get ready to play in August.

Fisher DeBerry from 1996 through 2006

1996 Air Force Falcons Coach Fisher DeBerry

The 1996 season and home opener was played on August 31, 1996 against San Jose State in Falcon Stadium Colorado Springs, CO. The Falcons shellacked and shutout the Spartans W (45-0). On Sep 7 at UNLV's Sam Boyd Stadium Las Vegas, NV, AFA pounded the Rebels W (65–17). Then, on Sep 21 at Wyoming's War Memorial Stadium Laramie, WY, the Cowboys beat the Falcons L (19–22). Then, on Sep 28 at home, the Falcons beat the Rice Owls W (45–17)

On Oct 12, at home, Navy beat the Falcons in the first game for the Commander-in-Chief's Trophy, L (17–20). On Oct 19 at Notre Dame in Notre Dame Stadium Notre Dame, IN, the Falcons defeated the Fighting Irish in a hard-fought overtime battle W (20–17) in OT. The highlights of this great win follow:

Oct 20, 1996
AIR FORCE 20, NOTRE DAME 17
https://www.washingtonpost.com/archive/sports/1996/10/20/air-force-20-notre-dame-17/3f5079cf-0645-46f8-b55c-49216cd9012e/?utm_term=.8d9c481fa496
Thank you to the Washington Post

Alex Pupich recovered Ron Powlus's fumble in overtime and Dallas Thompson kicked a 27-yard field goal as Air Force upset No. 8 Notre Dame, 20-17, today.

Thompson knelt to the ground as his kick sailed through the uprights, and his teammates surrounded him to celebrate. Several piled on him as the rest of the team traded hugs and high-fives. Notre Dame players, meanwhile, walked off the field with heads bowed after losing to the Falcons for the first time since 1985.

"We need to handle this with class," Notre Dame Coach Lou Holtz said. "Is it easy to take? No. We have no excuses."

Although it was Thompson's overtime field goal that won the game, it was Beau Morgan who engineered the victory. The senior quarterback rushed for a season-high 183 yards and a touchdown and completed 5 of 11 passes for 51 yards.

The Irish, meanwhile, couldn't get anything going. They were limited to 67 yards rushing.

Notre Dame got the ball first in overtime, but Powlus, back to throw, was hit by Joe Suhajda and had the ball stripped away. Pupich recovered at the Irish 25.

Notre Dame was called for a face-mask penalty, moving the Falcons to the Irish 10. After Todd Eilers rushed for two yards, Thompson came in for what would have been a 22-yard field goal attempt. As the kick sailed through the uprights, officials waved it off and penalized Air Force for delay of game. The five-yard penalty didn't matter as Thompson's second kick also was perfect.

The Falcons forced overtime when Morgan handed off to Tobin Ruff, who scampered 26 yards to tie the game at 17 with 7:15 left in regulation time. The score came five minutes after Marc Edwards had rushed a yard to break a 10-10 tie that had stood since halftime.

"Notre Dame made some big third-down plays, but in the fourth quarter, it was our team that made the plays," said Air Force Coach Fisher DeBerry. "I think that was the difference in the game."

Notre Dame looked as if it would come right back, as Robert Farmer returned the kickoff 24 yards to his 38. Powlus connected with Cikai Champion on a 29-yard pass, and Autry Denson ran for three yards to bring the Irish to the Falcons 30. But as Powlus went back to throw on second and seven, Pupich hit him and the ball tumbled out of his hand. Lee Guthrie recovered with six minutes left. Air Force got the ball twice more and Notre Dame once, but neither team could make anything happen before time ran out.

With the rushing game shut down, the Irish turned to the air. Powlus was 16 of 24 for 268 yards, but he either fumbled or was sacked when the Irish got close to the goal line.

Notre Dame's defense wasn't much help, either. With Morgan running the wishbone offense, the Falcons ran right through the Irish front seven, which entered the game 10th in the nation in total defense. Air Force finished with 304 yards rushing.

The lone bright spot for Notre Dame came when Allen Rossum returned Mel Whatley's punt 57 yards to put the Irish ahead 7-0 early in the first quarter. It was only the second punt return of Rossum's career, and the first came a few minutes earlier.

Rossum has now returned a punt, a kickoff and an interception for touchdowns.

Things went downhill for the Irish quickly after that. The Falcons responded with Thompson's 21-yard field goal, and Notre Dame was forced to punt on its next possession. Morgan rushed for 59 yards in the next series, including a five-yard scramble into the end zone to put the Falcons ahead 10-7 with 8:23 left in the half.

On Oct 26, 1996 at home, in Falcon Stadium, the Air Force beat Hawaii W (34–7). At home again on Nov 2, the Falcons were nosed out by Colorado State for the Ram–Falcon Trophy L (41–42). In the second service academy loss for AFA this season, on Nov 9 Army beat Air Force in Michie Stadium West Point, NY and gave up the Commander-in-Chief's Trophy L (7–23).

At Fresno State on Nov 16 in Bulldog Stadium, Fresno, CA, Air Force beat the Bulldogs in OT W (44–38). In the final game of the 1996 season. On Nov 28 at San Diego State in Jack Murphy Stadium, the Aztecs defeated the Falcons L (23–28).

1997 Air Force Falcons Coach Fisher DeBerry

The 1997 season and home opener was played on August 30, 1997 against Idaho in Falcon Stadium Colorado Springs, CO. The Falcons defeated, shellacked and shutout the Bengals W (14-10). At Rice on Sep 6 in Rice Stadium Houston, TX, the Falcons beat the Owls W (41–12). At home on Sep 13, the Falcons nosed out UNLV W (25–24). At Colorado State for the Ram-Falcon Trophy, on Sep 20 in Hughes Stadium Fort Collins, CO, the Falcons shutout the Rams W (24–0)

At home on Sep 27 the Air Force defeated San Diego State in OT, W (24–18). Then, on Oct 4 at home, the Falcons beat the Citadel by two touchdowns W (17–3). On Oct 11 at Navy in the Navy–Marine Corps Memorial Stadium Annapolis, MD for the Commander-in-Chief's Trophy, the Falcons beat the Midshipmen in a close match W (10–7_. At Falcon Stadium on Oct 18, Fresno State beat the Air Force L (17–20). Then, on Oct 25 at San Jose State's Spartan Stadium San Jose, CA, the Spartans defeated the Falcons L (22–25)

At Hawaii on Nov 1 in Aloha Stadium, Honolulu, HI the Falcons edged out the Rainbow Warriors W (34–27). On Nov 8 at home, Air Force defeated Army for this year's Commander-in-Chief's Trophy W (24–0). At home again on Nov 15, Air Force beat Wyoming W (14–3).

In the post-season on December 20, 1997, Air Force lost to Oregon in the Las Vegas Bowl at Sam Boyd Stadium Las Vegas, NV L((13–41)

Air Force was stung right in the beginning of the Las Vegas Bowl. Pat Johnson and Saladin McCullough literally stunned #23 Air Force by scoring on Oregon's first two plays from scrimmage. This was just the beginning as it kicked off a string of big plays leading the Ducks to a 41-13 victory in the Las Vegas Bowl.

Johnson, who was the 1995 Pac-10 400-meter champion, scored on passes of 69 and 78 yards and Tony Hartley caught two other RD passes for the Ducks, which dominated the first major bowl game of the season from the opening kickoff.

The game was just 18 seconds old when Johnson streaked down the left sideline to catch a pass in midstride from Akili Smith. He took it the full 69 yards from that point for a touchdown.

Right after Air Force was forced to punt, adding insult to injury, McCullough got the handoff up the middle on Oregon's next play from scrimmage and he took it 76 yards for another score to put the Ducks up 13-0 with only 2 minutes 6 seconds off the game clock.

Oregon led 26-0 at halftime, crushing Air Force's option offense and not allowing the Falcons to complete a pass until midway through the second quarter. Eventually the Falcons got over the sting, but the game had gotten by them by then.

It was the first win in the last five bowl games for the Ducks, who hadn't won a bowl game since beating Tulsa in the 1989 Independence Bowl.

Oregon took all of 69 seconds for its three offensive scores in the first half, the last coming on a five-play, 71-yard drive that put the Ducks up 26-0 on a 7-yard pass to Hartley in the end zone with 28 seconds left in the half.
The second half wasn't much different, with Oregon needing only 37 seconds for its first score and 42 seconds for another.

This game was billed as Oregon's potent offense against Air Force's stingy defense. But it became a lopsided encounter that forced Air Force (10-3) out of running its option offense in a futile effort to get anything going in the game. It was unusual for the Falcons for sure.

1998 Air Force Falcons Coach Fisher DeBerry

The 1998 season and home opener was played on September 5, 1998 against Wake Forest in Falcon Stadium Colorado Springs, CO. The Falcons defeated, shellacked and shutout Wake Forest W (42-10). At UNLV on Sep 12 in Sam Boyd Stadium, Whitney, Nevada the Falcons pounded the Rebels W (52–10). On Sep 17, at home, the Falcons edged out Colorado State for the Ram–Falcon Trophy, W

(30–27) on Sep 26 at TCU at the Amon G. Carter Stadium Fort Worth, Texas, the Horned Frogs nosed out the Falcons L (34–35)

On Oct at home, the Air Force smashed New Mexico W (56–14) At home on Oct 10, the Air Force crushed Navy for the Commander-in-Chief's Trophy W (49–7). At Tulsa, on Oct 24 at Skelly Stadium Tulsa, Oklahoma, the Falcons beat the Golden Hurricane W (42–21). On Oct 31 at home Air Force beat SMU W (31–7). At Army on Nov 7 in Michie Stadium West Point, New York, the Falcons beat the Black Knights for the Commander-in-Chiefs 1998 Trophy. W (35–7)

On Nov 14 at # 25 Wyoming, the #23 Falcons beat the cowboys at War Memorial Stadium Laramie, Wyoming, W (10–3). On Nov 21 at home, #20 Air Force defeated Rice W (22–16). On Dec 5 in the WAC Championship v BYU in Sam Boyd Stadium Whitney, Nevada, the #17 Falcons won the Championship W (20–13)

On Christmas day, Dec 25 v Washington on the Oahu Bowl # 16 Air Force defeated the Huskies in Aloha Stadium Honolulu, HI W (43–25)

Highlights of the Oahu Bowl

A lot of pundits see the major snub Air Force got from the Bowl Championship Committee by not being considered. In the Oahu Bowl, Air Force had something to prove to the Bowl Championship Series committee.

Having been snubbed in the national championship selection process despite an 11-1 record, the #16 ranked Falcons showed just how real they were by pounding the Washington Huskies 45-25 in the Oahu Bowl on Christmas Day.

Our sincere thank you to CBS News for this report on the game: https://www.cbsnews.com/news/air-force-flies-to-oahu-bowl-win/ The game, the back end of the first postseason bowl doubleheader -- Colorado upset No. 21 Oregon 51-43 in the Aloha Bowl -- was a rout in the second half.

Air Force coach Fisher DeBerry wants the BCS folks to know the Falcons are a Top 10 team.

"I'm at a loss for words right now," DeBerry said. "This is a team that people didn't think a whole lot of. People picked us to finish in the middle of our conference. The team got better and better. We lost a total of one game by one point."

"If this is not a Top 10 team, then I don't know what is."

With Blane Morgan deftly guiding the complex triple-option offense, the Falcons completed the day a little under their regular-season average on the ground with 232 yards and added another 267 passing.

"Our quarterback kept them off-balance all game long, "DeBerry said of Morgan's play. "Our offensive line did great, too."

The Falcons scored three of the first four times they had the ball to take a 22-13 lead at the half and got 16 unanswered points in the third quarter.

Morgan, not known as a prolific passer, even outplayed heralded Brock Huard, who plans to skip his final season to enter the NFL draft. The Air Force quarterback matched Huard's passing yardage, but did so on 11 fewer completions to go with a pair of touchdowns. Morgan also had 50 yards rushing.

"I feel disappointed," Huard said. "This is not the way I wanted to go out."

"Their success, their whole game was pressure. They moved their linemen all around. We couldn't pick them up really well. They executed, we didn't."

Huard's totals included no TDs and three interceptions.

"We made plays on offense, but couldn't catch up with them ,"Washington coach Jim Lambright said. "Our scout team we worked against didn't give us a picture the Air Force gave us on game day."

"You can't credit their quarterbacking and play-calling enough."

Said Morgan: "In practice, we had been throwing the ball as well as we had all year long. They (Washington) run a lot of guys up to the line to try to stop the run."

"It's a tremendous feeling. It's been a long road, a long four years.

Winning 12 games is a tremendous feeling."

Exactly a year ago, it was Lambright singing the praises of the Huskies, who demolished Michigan State 51-23 in the Aloha Bowl.

Air Force, which won its final nine games after a one-point loss to Texas Christian, used its quickness to bury the Huskies.

On its first three scores, Morgan guided Air Force on long drives -- 73, 83 and 74 yards -- with Jemal Singleton scoring twice, on runs of 12 and 2 yards, and Scott McKay getting the third on a 15-yard run.

The Falcons resorted to trickery on the third score, using a fake punt on fourth-and-8 -- a 10-yard run by Jason Sanderson -- to keep the ball moving.

Braxton Cleman scored on runs of 3 and 1 yards for Washington to make it 22-13 at the half, but the Falcons' big third quarter ended the Huskies' hopes.

The scores came on a 42-yard field goal by Jackson Whiting, a 4-yard run by Spanky Gilliam and Morgan's 79-yard pass to Matt Farmer.

Morgan closed out the Air Force scoring by teaming with McKay on a 30-yard pass in the fourth quarter. With the game out of hand, Washington's Marques Tuiasosopo scampered 7 yards for one TD and then passed 11 yards to Mikjo Austin with four seconds left.

© 1998 SportsLine USA, Inc. All rights reserved
First published on December 25, 1998
CBS Sportsline

1999 Air Force Falcons Coach Fisher DeBerry

The 1999 season and home opener was played on September 4, 1999 against Villanova in Falcon Stadium Colorado Springs, CO. The

Falcons defeated the Wildcats W (37-13). The last meeting v the Huskies was the Oahu Bowl. At Washington on Sep 18 at Husky Stadium Seattle, the Falcons beat the Huskies W (31–21). On Sep 25 at home, Wyoming beat Air Force L (7–10). At San Diego State, on Oct 2 in Qualcomm Stadium, the Falcons edged out the Aztecs W (23–22).

On Oct 9 at Navy in FedExField Landover, Maryland for the first leg of the Commander-in-Chief's Trophy, the Falcons beat the Midshipmen W (19–14). At home on Oct 16, Utah beat Air Force L (15–21). On Oct 30 at BYU's Cougar Stadium Provo, Utah, the Cougars beat the Falcons L (20–27) On Nov 6 at home, Air Force shut out Army and picked up the Commander-in-Chief's Trophy W (28–0).

On Nov 13 at home, Air Force defeated UNLV W (35–16). On Nov 18 at Colorado State's Hughes Stadium Fort Collins, Colorado for the Ram–Falcon Trophy, the Rams got the Prize L (21–41). On Nov 27, at New Mexico's University Stadium Albuquerque, New Mexico, in the season finale, the Lobos beat the Falcons L (28–33).
*Non-conference game. All times are in Mountain Time.

2000 Air Force Falcons Coach Fisher DeBerry

The 2000 season and home opener was played on September 2, 2000 against Cal-State Northridge in Falcon Stadium Colorado Springs, CO. The Falcons annihilated the Matadors W (37-13) before 50,166. At home on Sep 9, Air Force beat BYU W (32–12) before 45,277. At Utah on Sep 23 in Rice-Eccles Stadium Salt Lake City, UT, the Falcons edged out the Utes W (23–14) before 37,151.

On Sep 30 at UNLV's Sam Boyd Stadium Whitney, NV, the Rebels outplayed the Falcons L (13–34) before 22,321, At home on Oct 7, the Falcons beat the Midshipmen W (27–13) before 50,342. On Oct 14, at Wyoming's War Memorial Stadium Laramie, WY, the Falcons defeated the Cowboys W 51–34 before 15,452. On Oct 21, at home, New Mexico edged out the Air Force L (23–29) before 40,446.

On Oct 28 at Notre Dame in Notre Dame Stadium Notre Dame, IN, Notre Dame nosed out Air Force in OT L (31–34) before 80,232 in the Irish's newly expanded stadium. Air Force defeated Army on Nov 4 at

Michie Stadium West Point, NY W (41–27) before 41,287 for the commander-in-Chief's Trophy.

On Nov 11, at home, the Falcons neat the Rams of Colorado State for the Ram–Falcon Trophy in a close win W (44–40) before 35,151. At home again, on Nov 18, the Falcons pounded the Aztecs W (45–24) before 33,975

In the Silicon Valley Football Classic on December 31, 2000 vs. Fresno State in Spartan Stadium San Jose, CA, the Falcons edged out the Spartans W (37–34) before 26,542.

Highlights Silicon Valley Football Classic

Dean Martin once said that everybody loves somebody sometime. Well, let me say that everybody knows something sometime. For this game, the pundits believe that the Fresno State Bulldogs knew the Air Force Academy gets its kicks from blocking field goals, so they cooked up a plan just two weeks before game time to combat that potential opportunity for AFA.

When the time came to unveil the strategy, the Bulldogs were totally prepared, had everything lined up, and diagnosed the situation perfectly -- only their execution was more than a little nipper off.

The game had already brought back memories of those wild, high-scoring games of the WAC, but in this contest in a different conference, Air Force barely hung on for their 37-34 win over Fresno State in the inaugural Silicon Valley Football Classic at Spartan Stadium. AFA had it tough as almost all the fans were pro-Bulldogs out of a crowd of 26,542.

Their workaround was a fake FG that would not get blocked. Holder Jason Simpson, not a QB by trade could not hit an open Gianchino Chiaramonte in the end zone on the fake field goal try while tight end Donnell Burch was also open in back of the end zone.

At the time, there were just nine seconds left, robbing the Bulldogs of a chance to snatch a victory in what has to be one of the wildest contests of the bowl season. Fresno State had trailed by 27 at the half and it looked like the grim reaper had already cursed their efforts.

"That's the decision I made, and I have no second thoughts about it," said Fresno State coach Pat Hill. "We were going for the win. If anything, we just ran out of time. Most everybody thought it was going to overtime. Air Force is good at blocking kicks. We knew we were going to use it.

Air Force's Mike Thiessen (#3), prepares to throw a pass in Q2

"We just came up short. It was a well-conceived play. We believed it would work." Actually, the play was fairly simple. If the Falcons showed two "jumpers" -- players in the middle of the line whose role is to leap and try to bat the ball down -- holder Simpson would grab the ball away from kicker Ashen Asparuhov, drop back and pass to tight end Alec Greco, who'd be running across the middle. One jumper would mean a straight field-goal try.

When Air Force linebackers Corey Nelson and Kevin Runyon appeared to both be in jumper mode as the Bulldogs lined up for the 33-yard field goal, the chicanery was on. But Greco collided with Air Force's Paul Mayo at the line of scrimmage, was knocked down and never made it downfield. Simpson's second option (Chiaramonte) and third option (Burch) were also free, Simpson just couldn't hit his man, throwing the ball in between Chiaramonte and Burch. Chiaramonte was covered by Jeff Overstreet and had him beat.

Another tight end, Jeremy Johnson, was the ideal guy the Bulldogs wanted to use in that situation, but he suffered a stinger in the first quarter out was out of the contest. Otherwise, he would have been on the field instead of Greco.

"They're trying to make an old man out of me," said Air Force coach Fisher DeBerry. "I thought they'd try to kick the field goal. We had all 11 guys in position to field-goal block. That's why the guy was so wide-open. That's why the guy didn't complete the pass, he was shocked to see the guy wide-open."

Said Nelson: "The holder just takes off with the ball and I'm like, 'Oh, come on . . . At the time, I was pretty much helpless because I'm up in the air . . . so I'm not going to be able to get over there and help. Thank God for that guy not seeing the open receiver in back of the end zone."

The Falcons benefited from an apparent gaffe by Fresno State quarterback Daivd Carr. On third down from the Falcons' 16-yard line with 14 seconds left, Carr spiked the ball. And it wasn't a matter of brain-lock or forgetting what down it was, Carr knew exactly what he was doing. After a timeout, Fresno State went for the victory.

"I knew the (play) clock was ticking down, and I couldn't get the play (from the sideline) they wanted to run," said Carr, who threw for 391 yards and five touchdowns. "I didn't just want to throw it up. I knew we were in four-down territory, anyway. Everybody was jumping up and down, trying to be head coach. It was hard to see coach Hill for the play."

"I knew we had at least one more play. I knew it was either second or third down. All the guys were caught up in the moment of the game."

This contest was two games in one. Air Force rolled to a 34-7 lead in the first half, slicing, dicing and shredding the Bulldogs defense for 319 total yards. Quarterback Mike Thiessen ran for two touchdowns and passed for two more, both going to Bellarmine High of San Jose graduate Scotty McKay, and Dave Adams added a pair of field goals.

All the Bulldogs could manage was a 73- yard touchdown pass from Carr to Paris Gaines.

"We were a little dinged," Hill said. "Air Force really put it to us in all phases of the game. We were like a fighter (who got caught) with a good right hand. We were reeling. We took a standing eight count and came back in the second half.

Air Force 37; Fresno State 34. Now, that's a fine game. That's a great game to win for sure.

2001 Air Force Falcons Coach Fisher DeBerry

Air Force could not match its 9-3 play from 2000 and finished the 2001 season at 500 with a 6-6, 3-4 in Mountain West play to finish in a tie for fifth place. There would be no bowl game this year for the Falcons, though as usual they again played as hard as any team in the NCAA.

The 2001 season and home opener was played on September 1, 2001 at home against Oklahoma, always a US college football powerhouse. The game was played in AFA's home field of Falcon Stadium Colorado Springs, CO. The Sooners sucked all the air out of Falcon Stadium as Air Force found little opportunity to breathe in losing to the well-oiled Oklahoma boys L (3-44) before 56,162.

The Falcons came right back on Sep 8 at home v Tennessee Tech with a big shutout victory W (42–0) before 28,525. The AFA kept the muscle going on Sep 29 pounding San Diego State in Qualcomm Stadium San Diego, CA W (45–21) before 22,193. Then, on Oct 6 in a Navy home game, Air Force was triumphant at FedExField in Landover, MD W (24–18) putting the AFA in line for the Commander-in-Chief's Trophy before 36,251.

At home on Oct 13 the Air Force defeated Wyoming in Falcon Stadium W (24–13) before 44,258. By now Fisher DeBerry's good friend, LaVell Edwards had become a BYU immortal and had a stadium named after him. (hint, hint). On Oct 20 at BYU's LaVell Edwards Stadium Provo, UT, the Falcons had forgotten they could beat even the best BYU could throw at them and so Air Force was trounced by Brigham Young University like in the olden days L (33–63) before 62,382.

At New Mexico on Oct 27, at University Stadium Albuquerque, NM, the Lobos pounded Air Force for a victory L (33–52) before 28,047. Army was not winning many v Air Force in these days and 2001 would not be a game change. On Nov 3 at home, Army could not keep up with the Air Force and the Falcons took the win W (34–24) before 44,910, giving the AFA another Commander-in-Chief's Trophy win.

At Colorado State on Nov 8 in Hughes Stadium Fort Collins, CO for the Ram–Falcon Trophy, the Rams pulled off the victory L (21–28) before 26,638. On Nov 17 at home, UNLV slugged Air Force L (10–34) before 31,074. At Hawaii on November 24, in Aloha Stadium Honolulu, HI , the Falcons could not keep pace and lost L (30–52) before 41,148. With Air force looking anywhere for a win to break 500, the late fall encounter on Dec 1 against Utah at home, provided the perfect opportunity. The Falcons literally nosed out the Utes on Dec 1 W (38–37) before 25,702.

2002 Air Force Falcons Coach Fisher DeBerry

The 2002 season and home opener was played on August 31, 2002 at home against Northwestern from the Big Ten. The game was played in AFA's home field of Falcon Stadium Colorado Springs, CO. The Falcons overwhelmed the Wildcats W (52-3) before 45,114. At home on Sep 7, the Falcons beat New Mexico W (38–31) in OT 36,620. On Sep 21 # 23 California in California Memorial Stadium Berkeley, CA, the Falcons edged out the Golden Bears W (23–21) before 31,816. At Utah on Sep 28 in Rice-Eccles Stadium Salt Lake City, UT, the Falcons edged out the Utes W (30–26) before 35,659.

On Oct 5 at home, Air Force pounded Navy for the Commander-in-Chief's Trophy W (48–7) before 48,550. At home on Oct 12, the #21 Falcons shellacked BYU W (52–9) before 42,214. At home on Oct 19, #7 Notre Dame defeated Air Force L 14–21 before 56,409. On Oct 26 at Wyoming, the #22 Falcons lost to the Cowboys in War Memorial Stadium Laramie, WY, L (26–34) before 15,022. On Oct 31, the # 24 ranked Falcons lost to Colorado State at home for the Ram–Falcon Trophy L (12–31) before 39,063. At Army on Nov 9, the Falcons captured the Commander-in-Chief's Trophy in Michie Stadium West Point, NY W (49–30) before 39,288

At UNLV on Nov 16, in Sam Boyd Stadium Whitney, NV, the Falcons beat the Rebels W (49–32) before 25,417. Then, on Nov 23 at home, San Diego State beat Air Force L (34–38) before 31,023.

On December 31, 2002, at 8:30 p.m., #19 Virginia Tech edged out Air Force at Pacific Bell Park San Francisco, CA in the San Francisco Bowl L (13–20) before 25,966

San Francisco Bowl Highlights

(Provided by the Hokies)

SAN FRANCISCO - The Virginia Tech Hokies rallied from a 10-point deficit to take the lead in the second half and Ronyell Whitaker made two huge defensive plays in the waning seconds as the Hokies rang in the New Year with a 20-13 win over Air Force in the inaugural Diamond Walnut San Francisco Bowl in front of more than 25,000 fans at Pac Bell Park.

With the win, Tech finished the season 10-4, notching the sixth 10-win season in the program's history. As a program, the Hokies improved to 6-10 in bowl games, including a 5-5 mark in head coach Frank Beamer's tenure.

But perhaps more importantly, Tech's seniors notched their 40th win, making them the winningest class in school history.

"For these seniors, to go out as the all-time winningest class is pretty significant," Beamer said. "And now we're going to be second behind Michigan as far as being ranked in consecutive weeks in the top 25. We won 10 games. There were some great things that came out of this win over a really good Air Force team."

Tech trailed 10-0 in the first quarter, but rallied and took a 17-10 lead on a Lee Suggs' 1-yard touchdown run with 4:55 left in the first quarter. The two teams then traded field goals as the Hokies led 20-13 going into the game's final possession.

Air Force (8-5) took over at its own 18 with 4:11 left in the game and managed to drive deep into Tech territory. On first-and-20 from the

Tech 39, Air Force quarterback Chance Harridge tried to hit a wide-open Anthony Park, but Whitaker, Tech's senior cornerback, knocked the ball away at the last second to save a touchdown.

Three plays later, Air Force managed to convert a fourth-and-11 - the Falcons converted 4-of-5 fourth-down conversions in the game - when Harridge hit J.P. Waller for a 20-yard gain to the Tech 10. Two Harridge incompletions left the Falcons with seven seconds on the clock and basically time for one last play.

On the game's final play, Harridge dropped back to pass, but finding no one open, he tried to scramble for the end zone. Whitaker hit Harridge at the Tech 4, and Harridge, in desperate straits, heaved the ball toward offensive lineman Brett Huyser. Jason Murphy and Lamar Cobb buried Huyser to end the game, setting off a wild celebration on the Tech sideline.

"I was hoping that I wouldn't let a quarterback embarrass me," Whitaker said, laughing. "Nah, he's a great player and he was playing with an injury. He's a tough kid. I take nothing away from him.

"I had to make a play. If not, Coach Foster would have been on me, the fans would have been on me ... it would have been deja vous. I couldn't have picked a better way to end my career."

Tech's defense got off to a shaky start as Air Force jumped out to a 10-0 lead less than eight minutes into the game. On the Falcons' first possession, they went 80 yards in three minutes, thanks largely to a 47-yard pass play from Harridge to Park that got the Falcons to the Tech 27. Air Force scored on the drive when Matt Ward took the pitch on a reverse and went 15 yards for a score.

The Falcons then took advantage of a questionable Suggs' fumble - Suggs appeared to have hit the ground first and the ground cannot cause a fumble. Taking over at the Tech 35, Air Force ended up settling for a season-long 45-yard field goal by Joey Ashcroft.

But the Hokies settled down after that, allowing just three points the rest of the game. Air Force, which came into the nation ranked No. 1 in rushing offense (314.5 ypg), amassed just 227 yards on the ground.

And Harridge completed just 4-of-19 for 91 yards, with two interceptions.

Offensively, quarterback Bryan Randall, the game's offensive most valuable player, led the Hokies. Randall completed 18-of-23 for 177 yards, while Suggs led the Hokies rushing attack with 70 yards on 19 carries and two touchdowns. As a team, Tech finished with just 278 yards of total offense.

...

2003 Air Force Falcons Coach Fisher DeBerry

Air Force finished the 2003 season with a 7-5 record, 3-4 in Mountain West play. They finished in a three-way tie for fourth place. The Falcons were not invited to a bowl game this year. This would be the last winning season for Fisher DeBerry at Air Force as his next three years before retirement would be below 500.

The 2003 season and home opener was played on August 30, 2003 at home against Wofford, Fisher DeBerry's alma-mater. The game was played in AFA's home field of Falcon Stadium Colorado Springs, CO. The Falcons walloped the Terriers for the shutout victory W (49-0) before 40,111. Air Force nosed out Northwestern by one point on Sep 6 in Ryan Field Evanston, IL W (22–21) before 21,722. The next win for Air Force was against North Texas on Sep 13 at home W (34–21) before 32,541. At home again on Sep 20, Air Force defeated Wyoming W (35–29) before 38,622.

On Sep 27, Air Force defeated BYU in LaVell Edwards Stadium Provo, UT, W (24–10) before 62,210. On Oct 4, my wedding anniversary, at Navy, the #25 ranked Falcons lost the Commander-in-Chief's Trophy game to the Midshipmen L (25–28) before 30,623 in FedExField Landover, MD. On Oct 11, at home, Air Force beat UNLV W (24–7) before 43,873. Then, on Oct 16 at Colorado State in Hughes Stadium Fort Collins, CO, the Rams won the Ram–Falcon Trophy L (20–30) before 32,701. Then, on Nov 1 at home, Utah beat the Air Force L (43–45) in 3 OT periods before 30,004.

On Nov 8 the Air Force defeated Army at home in Falcon Stadium Colorado Springs, COW (31–3) before 50,108. Air Force won the Commander in Chiefs Trophy this year and it was the first of seven victories in a row for the Midshipmen. On Nov 15 at New Mexico, the Lobos beat the Falcons at University Stadium • Albuquerque, NM L (12–24) before 35,132. On Nov 22, Air Force lost its final game of the 2003 season at San Diego State in Qualcomm Stadium San Diego, CA L (3–24) before 23,682

2004 Air Force Falcons Coach Fisher DeBerry

The 2004 season and home opener was played on Sep 4, 2004 at home against #4 ranked California. The game was played in AFA's home field of Falcon Stadium Colorado Springs, CO. The Falcons were walloped by the Golden Bears L (14-56) before 50,075. At home on Sep 11, the falcons beat Eastern Washington W (42–20) before 34,389. At UNLV on Sep 18 in Sam Boyd Stadium Whitney, NV, the Falcons beat the Rebels W (27–10) before 23,823. Then, on Sep 25, #14 Utah defeated Air Force at Rice-Eccles Stadium Salt Lake City, UT L (35–49) before 44,043

At home, on Sep 30, Navy beat Air Force and won the Commander-in-Chief's Trophy L (21–24) before 44,279. Then, on Oct 9 at home, Air Force beat New Mexico W (28–23) before 36,369. At home on Oct 23, BYU beat Air Force L (24–41) before 38,235. Then, on Oct 30 at Wyoming's War Memorial Stadium in Laramie, WY, the Cowboys beat the Falcons L (26–43) before 13,716.

Air force beat Army on Nov 6 at Michie Stadium West Point, NY W (31–22) before 40,129. Navy won the Commander-in-Chief's Trophy. On Nov 13, at home, San Diego State edged out Air Force L (31–37) before 28,514. Air Force won the Rem-Falcon Trophy game this year on Nov 20, defeating Colorado State in a one-sided game W (47–17) before 34,441 to wrap up the 2004 season.

2005 Air Force Falcons Coach Fisher DeBerry

The 2005 season opener was played on September 3, 2005 against Washington in Qwest Field • Seattle, WA. The Falcons edged out the Huskies W (20-17) before 26,482. On Sep 10, at home, Air Force beat San Diego State W (41–29) before 30,101.

At home on Sep 23, Wyoming beat Air Force L (28–29) before 41,240. On Sep 22 at Utah's Rice-Eccles Stadium Salt Lake City, UT, the Utes edged out the Falcons L (35–38) before 41,935.

On Sep 29 at Colorado State's Hughes Stadium Fort Collins, CO for the Ram–Falcon Trophy, the Rams beat the Falcons L (23–41) before 26,711. At Navy on Oct 8 in Navy–Marine Corps Memorial Stadium Annapolis, MD for the Commander-in-Chief's Trophy, Navy beat Air Force L (24–27) before 35,211. Then, on Oct 15, at home, Air Force pounded UNLV W (42–7) before 30,573.

On Oct 22, at home, # 21 TCU walloped Air Force L (10–48) before 33,210. At BYU on Oct 29, the Cougars thumped the Falcons at LaVell Edwards Stadium Provo, UT L (41–62) before 57,687. At home v Army, on Nov 5, the Black Knights edged out the Falcons giving Navy the Commander-in-Chief's Trophy, L (24–27) before 44,782. On Nov 19, in the final game of the season, at New Mexico's University Stadium Albuquerque, NM, the Falcons beat the Lobos W 42–24 before 33,791.

2006 Air Force Falcons Coach Fisher DeBerry

DeBerry announced his retirement following the conclusion of the season. They were a member of the Mountain West Conference. They finished the season 4–8, 3–5 in Mountain West play to finish in a tie for sixth place.

The 2006 season opener was played on September 9, 2006 against #11 Tennessee in Neyland Stadium Knoxville, TN. L 30-31 The Volunteers edged out the Falcons L (30-31 before 105,466. On Sep 23 at Wyoming's War Memorial Stadium Laramie, WY, the Falcons beat the Cowboys W 31–24 before 20,177.

Then, on Sep 30, at home, the Air Force beat New Mexico W (24–7) before 40,453. Then, on Oct 7, at home, Navy beat the Air Force to take the first leg of the Commander-in-Chief's Trophy L (17–24) before 45,246.

On Oct 12, at home, Colorado State won the Ram–Falcon Trophy W (24–21) before 30,008. On Oct 21 at San Diego State in Qualcomm Stadium San Diego, CA, the Aztecs beat the Falcons L (12–19) before 26,871. On Oct 28 at home BYU beat Air Force L (14–33) before

35,521. Then, on Nov at Army's Michie Stadium West Point, NY, Air Force pounded the Army squad W (43-7) Navy won the Commander-in-Chief's Trophy before 32,066.

At home on Nov 11, #9 Notre Dame beat the Air Force L (17–39) before 49,367. At home again on Nov 18 Utah edged out the Falcons L (14–17) before 27,611. On Nov 24 at Sam Boyd Stadium Whitney, NV UNLV edged out the Air Force L (39–42) before 13,927. Two weeks later in the final game of the season and Fisher DeBerry's last game, on Dec 2, TCU knocked off Air Force at Amon G. Carter Stadium Fort Worth, TX L (14–38) before 30,767

Fisher DeBerry—an Epilogue

I admit though I never met Fisher DeBerry personally that I am a little choked up about not being able to write about his great exploits as a coach on the football field. DeBerry is alive and in great health as I write this epilogue as the second-last section of this book about Air Force. Not only is he alive, he is doing well, and as one author Bill Wagner recently noted DeBerry is leading a charmed life.

Right after we finish with this fine article about DeBerry, for which we thank Mr. Wagner, we will look at his latest recognition—membership in the Hall of fame. We'll then pick up with Troy Calhoun's thirteen years of exploits as the Air Force mentor. Enjoy.

Legendary Air Force head coach Fisher DeBerry leading charmed life

Fisher DeBerry was once the undisputed champion of service academy football, leading Air Force to 17 winning seasons and 12 bowl berths while serving as head coach from 1984 through 2006. We also included images by Brian Bahr / Getty Images as they were presented in the article.

Here is a picture of Mr. Wagner.
Bill Wagner
Contact Reporterbwagner@capgaznews.com

Fisher DeBerry readily admits he leads a charmed life these days.

DeBerry and his wife, LuAnn, spend six months in Grove, Oklahoma – nearby to their two children and eight grandchildren. They spend the other half of the year in Isle of Palms, South Carolina, at the retirement home they built that overlooks the Atlantic Ocean.

Together, the couple devotes considerable time and effort to the Fisher DeBerry Foundation, which is dedicated to the support and education of single mothers and their children. That is a cause that is very personal to DeBerry, who grew up without a father in the country town of Cheraw, S.C.

"I was a single-parent kid and I don't know what I would have done without my coaches," said DeBerry, who was honored to give the eulogy at the funerals of the three men who served as important mentors. That would be the Cheraw High football and baseball coach along with Wofford football coach Jim Brakefield.

DeBerry travels around the country speaking at fundraising events for the foundation, which annually sends 500 to 600 youngsters to summer camps. He relies on connections developed during a 44-year college football coaching career to get notable names from his lifelong profession to work those camps.

"We believe if we can get these kids to a camp so they be around the right kind of people and learn a little about leadership, character and integrity it can make a difference in their lives," DeBerry said. DeBerry was once the undisputed champion of service academy football, leading Air Force to 17 winning seasons and 12 bowl berths while serving as head coach from 1984 through 2006. The Falcons captured the coveted Commander-in-Chief's Trophy 14 times during the 21-year tenure of DeBerry, who was a combined 34-8 against Army and Navy.

Now DeBerry is a fan of all the service academy programs, rooting almost as hard for Army and Navy as he does for Air Force. He was absolutely thrilled when the Black Knights, Falcons and Midshipmen all posted winning records and earned bowl berths in 2016.

The United States Naval Academy football season is underway. These are their opponents and who to look for.

"I'm so happy to see Air Force, Army and Navy football all on solid footing," DeBerry said during a phone interview with The Baltimore Sun Media Group on Thursday. "I'm not surprised because all three programs are being led by outstanding football coaches and fine men."

Of course, DeBerry has a special fondness for current Air Force head coach Troy Calhoun, who was a former player and assistant. Calhoun, a former starting quarterback for the Falcons, was tabbed to succeed DeBerry after he retired.

For the most part, Calhoun has continued the successful tradition established by DeBerry, leading Air Force to eight winning seasons capped by bowl berths during a 12-year tenure.

"I was tickled to death when Troy was selected. It was a great compliment to the program that an alum and former player was hired," DeBerry said. "Troy has done a fantastic job as I knew he would."

Air Force captured the coveted Commander-in-Chief's Trophy 14 times during the 21-year tenure of Fisher DeBerry, who was a combined 34-8 against Army and Navy. (DAVID ZALUBOWSKI / Associated Press)

However, DeBerry is just as complimentary of Army head coach Jeff Monken and Navy head coach Ken Niumatalolo, both of whom were once bitter rivals. Monken has resurrected the Black Knights in much the same way his former boss, Paul Johnson, did the Midshipmen.

Army currently holds the Commander-in-Chief's Trophy after sweeping Air Force and Navy in 2017. Monken, a Navy assistant under Johnson from 2002 through 2007, is looking to lead the Black Knights to their third straight winning season.

"Jeff understood what it took to succeed at a service academy and has really turned things around at Army," said DeBerry, who sent Monken a congratulatory letter after he was hired as head coach at West Point.

"I was really surprised to get that note. It was very classy of coach to send that note of good luck," Monken recently told the Colorado Springs-Gazette.

Meanwhile, Niumatalolo followed in the footsteps of Johnson and took Navy to even greater heights. The Midshipmen have posted winning records in 14 of the last 15 seasons while claiming the Commander-in-Chief's Trophy 10 times since 2003.

"Kenny has done such a tremendous job and is such a great person. He runs a first-class program," DeBerry said. "We love all those guys and admire what they're doing. They do it the right way and for the right reasons."

Former Air Force football coach DeBerry picked for Hall of Fame

Fisher DeBerry

*By IRV MOSS | imoss@denverpost.com |
PUBLISHED: May 17, 2011 at 3:56 pm |
UPDATED: May 3, 2016 at 10:00 am*

Fisher DeBerry made a significant addition to an already impressive resume when the former Air Force coach's selection to the College Football Hall of Fame was announced Tuesday by the National Football Foundation. DeBerry's class of new Hall of Famers will be inducted Dec. 6 at the Waldorf Astoria in New York.

"I'm overwhelmed and overjoyed," DeBerry, 72, said from his home in Isle of Palms, S.C. "I'm very happy for the recognition it brings to the Air Force Academy. We had one rule for everybody in our program and that was to do what was right. We asked them to make that commitment and they did."

DeBerry is the winningest coach in the history of service-academy football, compiling a 169-109-1 record with the Falcons from 1984-2006. Since his retirement from coaching, he has been active in charity work across the country with his Fisher DeBerry Foundation. The most recent event was Friday, a Colorado Coaches for Charity fundraiser at Invesco Field at Mile High.

DeBerry was selected for Hall of Fame induction in his first year on the ballot. He said he celebrated the announcement by attending a high school baseball game and having a barbecue dinner.

"I'm really pleased and happy for Fisher," said former Colorado State coach Sonny Lubick, like DeBerry a member of the Colorado Sports Hall of Fame. "He did a lot for college football, and this is well deserved."

Lubick shared a table with DeBerry at Friday's fundraiser, which attracted a crowd of nearly 300.

Seventeen of DeBerry's 23 Air Force teams finished with a winning record and he was 6-6 in bowl games. He was the national coach of the year in 1985, when the Falcons roared to a 10-0 start and finished 12-1, leading the nation in wins after beating Texas 24-16 in the Blue-bonnet Bowl in Houston. DeBerry coached another 12-1 team in 1998. The Falcons completed that season with a 45-25 rout of Washington in the Oahu Bowl in Honolulu.

DeBerry's 1985, 1995 and 1998 teams won Western Athletic Conference championships.

DeBerry came to Air Force in 1980 as an assistant coach on Ken Hatfield's staff. He was instrumental in helping Hatfield install the wishbone offense that fueled the Falcons' return to prominence.

After Hatfield left the Falcons to coach Arkansas, his alma mater, DeBerry was promoted to head coach by AFA athletic director Col. John Clune. The DeBerry-coached Falcons went 8-4 in 1984 and beat Virginia Tech 23-7 in the Independence Bowl in Shreveport, La.

One of the players DeBerry coached, 1987 Outland Trophy winner Chad Hennings, is a member of the College Football Hall of Fame.

Joining DeBerry in the 2011 class are coach Lloyd Carr, Michigan; Florida receiver Carlos Alvarez, Texas defensive lineman Doug English, Oregon State fullback Bill Enyart, Ohio State running back and Heisman Trophy winner Eddie George, Alabama defensive lineman Marty Lyons, Miami defensive lineman Russell Maryland, Florida State defensive back Deion Sanders, Georgia defensive back Jake Scott, Nebraska guard Will Shields, Minnesota quarterback Sandy Stephens, West Virginia linebacker Darryl Talley, Oklahoma halfback Clendon Thomas, Arizona defensive lineman Rob Waldrop and Michigan State receiver Gene Washington.

Irv Moss: 303-954-1296 or imoss@denverpost.com

Chapter 11 Coach Troy Calhoun 2007-2016

Calhoun   Coach # 7

Year	Coach	Record	Conference	Record
2007	Troy Calhoun	9–4	6–2	
2008	Troy Calhoun	8–5	5–3	
2009	Troy Calhoun	8–5	5–3	
2010	Troy Calhoun	9–4	5–3	
2011	Troy Calhoun	7–6	3–4	
2012	Troy Calhoun	6–7	5–3	
2013	Troy Calhoun	2–10	0–8	
2014	Troy Calhoun	10–3	5–3	
2015	Troy Calhoun	8–6	6–2	
2016	Troy Calhoun	10–3	5–3	

Calhoun to replace DeBerry at Air Force
Dec 22, 2006
Associated Press -- Our thinks to the AP for this piece

AIR FORCE ACADEMY, Colo. -- Former Air Force starting quarterback Troy Calhoun will replace Fisher DeBerry as head coach of the Falcons.

[It is always a better deal for a new coach or a new manager of a corporate office to know that the person they were replacing was not well likes and they would not have to be concerned about the comments post facto about their abilities compared to the former beloved mentor.

Think of Knute Rockne and how nobody else could replace him until somebody did. The same problem came with Troy Calhoun in his difficult role of replacing the still legendary Fisher DeBerry as the head coach of Air Force Football.

The best thing DeBerry did for the future of the program post-Deberry is to somehow have a tough couple seasons—much unlike his 23 others near the end of his career. Would DeBerry have gotten 9 wins out of his Juniors from 2006? Who knows? Actually nobody cares. Calhoun was a literal phenomenon and his finest credential was he was one of DeBerry's boys.]

Calhoun, who started for DeBerry in 1986, had been an assistant coach with the Denver Broncos before joining Gary Kubiak as offensive coordinator of the Houston Texans this season. Calhoun is a 1989 Air Force graduate -- the first former Air Force player to coach the Falcons.

"Our thought going into this was Fisher DeBerry had been here for 27 years, head coach for 23. And during that time he has inspired, trained, taught, motivated, produced not just leaders for the Air Force but leaders for the NCAA athletic community," Air Force athletic director Hans Mueh said during a news conference.

"Troy Calhoun I believe is at the pinnacle of that group of folks Fisher DeBerry produced and so we are proud that he would accept this offer from us to be our next head coach," he said.

Calhoun replaces DeBerry, who retired Dec. 15. Calhoun is only the sixth head coach for Air Force, joining a list that includes Bill Parcells and Ken Hatfield.

Calhoun, 38, began his coaching career with Air Force and continued at Ohio University and Wake Forest.

He caught on with the Broncos in 2003 as a defensive assistant and became an offense-special teams assistant in 2004. Last season, his title was "assistant to the head coach" for Mike Shanahan.

"Ultimately, this came down to deep down, in the heart, inside that chest cavity, you realize that hey, this is the academy and here's a chance to go back and coach and work with the kids and at the same time get a chance to probably cross paths with a few more teammates and old friends, too," Calhoun said of his decision to leave the NFL.

"It's a place where as a graduate you're extremely proud to return in whatever capacity."

Calhoun, who had talked with DeBerry before the selection, will remain with the Texans during the remaining two games of their season.

The 68-year-old DeBerry finished with three straight losing seasons and two big controversies in his final years.

"I think Troy is going to reinstill the kind of fire and passion that has been missing over the past couple of years," Mueh said, without elaborating.

DeBerry spent 27 years at the school, including four as an assistant coach. His 169-109-1 record made him the winningest coach in Air Force history and he had the third-longest tenure at one school of any active college coach, after Joe Paterno (41 years at Penn State) and Bobby Bowden (31 years at Florida State).

Calhoun also has some big shoes to fill in the Commander-in-Chief's trophies awarded to the winner of the annual service academy rivalry. DeBerry was 35-11 against Army and Navy and led Air Force to 14 trophies, though he lost his grip on the trophy as Navy won it the last four years.

But DeBerry also had problems off the field in recent years.
In 2005, he was criticized after a 48-10 loss to TCU when he said Air Force didn't have enough "Afro-American" players, singling

them out for being able to run well. DeBerry was reprimanded by top brass at the academy and offered a public apology.

In 2004, academy officials asked him to remove a banner from the locker room that included the lines "I am a Christian first and last ... I am a member of Team Jesus Christ."

During his nine-minute farewell news conference, DeBerry mentioned his faith, thanking "my Master Coach for leading us to Colorado 26 years ago."

Calhoun is quite a guy to get DeBerry's endorsement

2007 Air Force Falcons Coach Troy Calhoun

The Air Force Falcons football team represented the United States Air Force Academy in the 2007 college football season playing as a Division I-A MWC. They played their home games in Falcon Stadium in Colorado Springs, CO. It was their fifty-third season of inter-collegiate football. They were led by coach Troy Calhoun in his first season with Air Force.

Troy Calhoun was announced as the new AFA coach shortly after Coach DeBerry offered his retirement following the conclusion of the 2006 season. The Falcons were a member of the Mountain West Conference. They finished the season 9-4, 6-2 in Mountain West play to finish in second place. Troy Calhoun coached the Falcons to their first winning season since 2003. They were invited to the Armed Forces Bowl where they lost to California.

The 2007 season and home opener was played on September 1, 2007 against South Carolina in Falcon Stadium Colorado Springs, CO. The Falcons pounded the Bulldogs W (34-3) before 39,364. On Sep 8 at Utah in Rice-Eccles Stadium Salt Lake City, UT, the Falcons beat the Utes W (20–12) before 43,454. On Sep 13, the Air Force edged out TCU at home W (20–17) in OT before 31,556. At nemesis BYU, on Sep 22, in LaVell Edwards Stadium Provo, UT, the Cougars beat the Falcons before 64,502.

At Navy on Sep 29, in Navy–Marine Corps Memorial Stadium Annapolis, MD, the Midshipmen beat the Falcons L 20–31 before

37,615. Then, on Oct 6, at home, the Falcons beat UNLV W (31–14) before 35,583. At Colorado State, on Oct 13 in Hughes Stadium Fort Collins, CO for the Ram–Falcon Trophy, Air Force prevailed W (45–21) before 25,150. On Oct 20 at home, AFA beat Wyoming W (20–12) before 41,531. At New Mexico on Oct 25 in University Stadium Albuquerque, NM, the Lobos squeaked out a win v AFA L (31–34) before 26,087

At home on Nov 3. The Falcons whipped the Army W (30–10) before 46,144. Navy won the Commander-in Chief's Trophy. On Nov 10 at Notre Dame in Notre Dame Stadium • Notre Dame, IN, the Falcons defeated the Fighting Irish in what some would say was a rout W (41–24). The Falcons were on the prowl and Notre Dame was a great catch for Air Force. The game was played before 80,795. On Nov 17, the Falcons whooped San Diego State at home in a blowout W (55–23) before 34,227

In the post-season, on December 31, 2007 at 10:30 a.m. v California in Amon G. Carter Stadium Fort Worth, TX for the Armed Forces Bowl, the Falcons looked in good form but lost the game on a one-TD difference L 36–42 before 40,905

Highlights of the Armed Services Bowl.

The Air Force had gone into a slump on bowl games in the last four years of Fisher DeBerry's time and few thought a new couch would produce such a resurrection at Air Force. But, Troy Calhoun pulled off what would have been considered impossible.

And, so, the impossible became the improbable and then it became a fait accompli as Air Force fooled everybody and like Mark Twain, they proved that the rumors of their death had been greatly exaggerated—and then some.

Getting a bowl day bid would have been impossible with a bad record but the new Air Force Coach was like a new Fisher DeBerry who would never say no. He not only made the pundits question their punditry in 2007, he produced a great Air Force Squad that made it because of great play to the Armed Services Bowl. They were ready though they faced a determined and competent opponent.

The opponent was the Golden Bears of California. They came out for the game without last names on the backs of their uniforms. This was change from their look throughout the season. Prior to the game, Golden Bears players kick returner DeSean Jackson, wide receiver Robert Jordan, and free safety Thomas DeCoud had been suspended for the first quarter of the game for violating team rules. A few wild and crazy players had violated the rules but would be back in before half-time.

The Falcons started tough. The Golden Bears struggled early against AFA. Like most squads, The Bears had trouble in the early going of the game adjusting to the Falcons triple option offense and unpredictable line formations.

Golden Bears quarterback Nate Longshore started in the first quarter, but was hampered by the absence of DeSean Jackson and Robert Jordan. Longshore completed 5 of 8 passes for 36 yards in the first quarter.

As Cal coach Jeff Tedford had planned, backup quarterback Kevin Riley took over for Longshore in the second quarter. Riley completed two touchdown passes to DeSean Jackson and Lavelle Hawkins to make it 21–14 Falcons at the half. The game was not decided yet.

Falcons Carney suffered a gruesome lower body injury in the third quarter on a running play and did not return. Backup Shea Smith, who had not played all year, replaced Carney. The Falcons were then limited to a pair of field goals, while Robert Jordan caught a pass for a touchdown and Justin Forsett ran in for one.

In the fourth quarter, things did not improve much for Air Force. Forsett rushed for another score in the fourth quarter, as did Riley. Air Force was limited to field goals until they capitalized on a botched kickoff return to score a touchdown with just over two minutes left, but as most teams in futility, the failed to recover an onside kick.

During the game, Carney finished with one touchdown pass and 108 yards rushing. Alongside Carney, Falcons running back Jim Ollis also eclipsed the 100-yard rushing mark with 101, while Forsett had 140. Riley completed 269 passing yards and was the game MVP. But, the bottom line is that AFA could not get it all together and lost the Armed Services Bowl by --- just six points.

2008 Air Force Falcons Coach Troy Calhoun

The Air Force Falcons football team represented the United States Air Force Academy in the 2008 college football season playing as a Division I-A MWC. They played their home games in Falcon Stadium in Colorado Springs, CO. It was their fifty-fourth season of intercollegiate football. They were led by coach Troy Calhoun in his second season with Air Force.

Troy Calhoun was announced as the new AFA coach shortly after Coach DeBerry offered his retirement following the conclusion of the 2006 season. His first year was his best year so far but his subsequent years such as this year were also good. The Falcons were a member of the Mountain West Conference. They finished the season 8-5, 5-3 in Mountain West play to finish in fourth place. Troy Calhoun coached the Falcons to their second consecutive winning season. They finish in fourth place in the MWC. They were invited to the Armed Forces Bowl where they lost to Texas.

The 2008 season and home opener was played on Aug 30, 2008 against Southern Utah in Falcon Stadium Colorado Springs, CO. The Falcons drubbed the Thunderbirds W (41-7) before 39,180. On Sep 6 at Wyoming's War Memorial Stadium Laramie, WY, Calhoun's Falcons on handily W (23–3) before 23,168. On Sep 13 at Houston in Gerald Ford Stadium , Dallas, TX, the Falcons edged out the Cougars W (31–28) before 2,546. On Sep 20 at home, #20 Utah edged out the Falcons L (23–30) before 36,952.

Then, at home on Oct 4, Navy got the best of Air Force for the Commander-in-Chief's Trophy L (27–33) before 46,339, At san Diego State on Oct 11 in Qualcomm Stadium San Diego, CA the Falcons beat the Aztecs W (35–10) before 43,630. On Oct 18 at UNLV in Sam Boyd Stadium Whitney, NV, Air Force squeaked out a victory by one point over the Rebels W (29–28) before 21,055. At home against the Lobos on Oct 23, the Falcons beat New Mexico W (23–10) before 25,101. At Army on Nov 1, Air Force beat the Black Knights W (16-7) before 37,409. Navy won the Commander-in-Chief's Trophy for the sixth straight year in 2008.

On Nov 8, at home, Air Force beat Colorado State W (38–17) before 39,052. In a losing effort at home v BYU on Nov 15, the Cougars beat the Falcons L (24-38 before 42,177. At #16 TCU on Nov 22 in Amon G. Carter Stadium Fort Worth, TX, the Horned Frogs trounced the Falcons L (10–44) before 32,823.

On December 31, 2008. At 10:00 a.m., Houston beat Air Force in Amon G. Carter Stadium Fort Worth, TX in the Armed Forces Bowl L (28–34) before 41,127

Dec 31 Armed Services Bowl Highlights

Armed Forces Bowl puts military might on display
By Marine Lance Cpl. Bryan G. Carfrey January 2, 2009

FORT WORTH, Texas -- The sixth annual Bell Helicopter Armed Forces Bowl football game featured the Houston Cougars (7-5) taking on the U.S. Air Force Academy Falcons (8-4) on Dec. 31 at the Amon G. Carter Stadium here.

Kickoff for the Armed Forces Bowl was noon Eastern, but the event started more than 24-hours prior to the kickoff when both teams were welcomed to Fort Worth with a luncheon at the Fort Worth Convention Center on Dec. 30.

Retired Army Lt. Col. Greg Gadson, who survived severe injuries following a road-side bomb attack while deployed to Iraq, was the keynote speaker. Colonel Gadson was credited by the New York Giants football team for giving them the inspiration to turn their 0-2 season start into a Superbowl-winning season.

Outside the stadium, home of Texas Christian University's Horned Frogs, there was an "Adventure Zone" set up featuring almost 60 displays of military might from all the armed services.

"My son loves all the guns and tanks and we've had a really good time; it is wonderful here," said Ali Rattan, one of the spectators of the Adventure Zone on Dec. 30.

"A lot of people are coming out to see what the different services have to offer, and we get to put on display some of the equipment they have never seen before," said Marine Cpl. John Luis, an artillery cannoneer.

"They get to ask a lot of questions and we get to interact with them, it's really an awesome event."

The day's events was closed out by a pep rally for both teams culminating in a 10-minute fireworks display.

Prior to the game start on Dec. 31, pre-game festivities included a skydiving demonstration by a combined team of different types of Army paratroopers, and an Air Force flyover that included two F-16 Fighting Falcons and a B-52 Stratofortress. Army Gen. David Petraeus, U.S. Central Command commander, flanked by all of the senior service representatives, performed the coin toss.

"It just makes me absolutely proud to be here, it's a phenomenal event," said Army Maj. Gen. Peter M. Vangjel, commanding general of the United States Fires Center and Fort Sill, Okla., who was the senior Army official at the game. "It's nice to stop and think about all the folks in the armed forces, the impact we have on the nation, and to celebrate together with all the other services."

More than 40,000 tickets sold for the bowl game.

"It's a terrific opportunity, and not just for the Air Force, said Air Force Chief of Staff, Gen. Norton Schwartz. "We are representing the entire joint team -- Army, Navy, certainly the Air Force, and the Marines."

The halftime ceremonies included General Petraeus receiving the Great American Patriot of the Year Award from Tom Dials, chief executive officer of Armed Forces Insurance, and an oath of enlistment ceremony officiated by General Patraeus for more than 100 future servicemembers from all branches of service. The Air Force Academy's Wings of Blue parachute team ended the ceremony with their aerial demonstration.

During each quarter of the game, Armed Forces Bowl officials also spotlighted a different branch of service by running public service announcements on the "Jumbotron."

For the bowl game itself, Air Force lost to Houston, 34-28.

2009 Air Force Falcons Coach Troy Calhoun

The 2009 season and home opener was played on Sep 5, 2009 against Nicholls State in Falcon Stadium Colorado Springs, CO. The Falcons shellacked the Colonels W (72-0) in a shutout before 42,205. On Sep 12 at Minnesota in TCF Bank Stadium Minneapolis, MN, the Gophers beat the Falcons L (13–20) before 50,805. Then, on Sep 19 at New Mexico's University Stadium Albuquerque, NM, the Falcons defeated the Lobos W (37–13) before 26,246. At home v San Diego State, the Falcons defeated the Aztecs W (26–14) before 35,929.

At Navy on Oct 3 in Navy–Marine Corps Memorial Stadium Annapolis, MD for Navy's seventh (Commander-in-Chief's Trophy, the Midshipmen defeated the Falcons L (13–16) in OT before 37,820. On Oct 10, #9 TCU beat Air Force L (17–20) before 30,104. At home, on Oct 17, the Falcons beat the Cowboys of Wyoming in a close shutout W (10–0) before 34,117. At #20 Utah, on Oct 24 in Rice-Eccles Stadium Salt Lake City, UT, the Utes beat the Falcons L (16–23) in OT before 45,129

At Colorado State on Oct 31, in Hughes Stadium Fort Collins, CO for the Ram–Falcon Trophy, the Falcons beat the Rams W (34–16) before 22,025. At home on Nov 7 Air Force beat Army W (35-7) before 46,212. At home on Nov 14, Air Force beat UNLV W (45–17) before 25,370. In the regular season closer, on Nov 21, #13 BYU beat Air Force L (21-38) at LaVell Edwards Stadium Provo, UT before 64,071.

Then, on December 31, 2009, at 10:00 a.m. v # 25 Houston in Amon G. Carter Stadium Fort Worth, TX the Falcons pounded the Cougars in the Armed Forces Bowl W (47–20) before 41,414.

2009 Armed Services Bowl Highlights

https://www.sandiegouniontribune.com/sdut-air-force-picks-off-bowl-victory-over-houston-2009dec31-story.html

An appreciative Thank You to the San Diego Union-Tribune

Air Force picks off bowl victory over Houston

STEPHEN HAWKINS, AP Sports Writer

Air Force running back Jared Tew (42) carries the ball into the end zone to score as Houston cornerback Carson Blackmon (23), line backer C.J. Cavness (40), and safety Nick Saenz (41) defend during the first half of the Armed Forces Bowl NCAA college football game on Thursday, Dec. 31, 2009, in Fort Worth, Texas. (AP Photo/Tom Pennington) (/ AP)

With Asher Clark and Jared Tew grinding out yards and Air Force controlling the ball for more than 41 minutes, there were few chances for Case Keenum and Houston's potent offense.

Then when Keenum got on the field in the Armed Forces Bowl, he was often under pressure or getting picked off - or both.

Air Force's top-ranked pass defense had six interceptions and Clark and Tew each ran for more than 100 yards and two touchdowns to lead the Falcons to a 47-20 victory on Thursday.

"The front three kind of got in his head, kind of got into him," said safety Chris Thomas, who had two interceptions along with his 12 tackles. "When he was on the run like that, we feel like we had the advantage."

Houston quarterback Case Keenum (7) looks for an open receiver against Air Force during the first half of Armed Forces Bowl NCAA college football game, Thursday, Dec. 31, 2009, in Fort Worth, Texas. (AP Photo/Tom Pennington) (/ AP)

After the Falcons (8-5) went ahead on Clark's 36-yard TD to cap the opening drive of the game, Keenum's first pass attempt deflected off his falling receiver and was grabbed by Anthony Wright, who had three interceptions. That set up Tew's 6-yard TD run for a 14-0 lead.

When it was over, Keenum had thrown a career-high six picks and was 24 of 41 for a season-low 222 yards for the Cougars (10-4). Before throwing three interceptions with five TDs and a school-record 56 completions in a loss to East Carolina in the Conference USA championship game last month, Keenum had only six picks the first 12 games this season.

"Give Air Force all the credit and I'll take all the blame," Keenum said, opening a 78-second postgame statement before walking off without taking questions. "I'm going to learn from this. You know, I'm a winner and I'm a competitor. ... We're going to take this into the offseason and we're going to use it as motivation. Look for the Cougars to do something special next year because there's a lot of guys in this locker room who have got a lot of determination. "

The junior quarterback who played his 40th career game had previously said he plans to be back next season, when the Cougars return nine offensive starters, including three 1,000-yard receivers.

Keenum finished this season with a nation-leading 5,671 yards with 44 touchdowns and 15 interceptions.

"I'm not going to make any kind of generalization based on the overall numbers in the past two games for him," coach Kevin Sumlin said. "He's a damn good player. Has been, and will continue to be. ... He wasn't sharp today. We weren't sharp today at all."

Air Force ran for 402 yards and Tim Jefferson was effective through the air, hitting 10 of 14 passes for 161 yards.

"We felt that if we just kept doing what we do and the plays were called right, they couldn't stop us," said Tew, who finished with 26 carries for 173 yards. He had a 71-yard TD run with 3:32 left in the game after Keenum's fifth interception.

Clark ran 17 times for 129 yards for the Falcons, who had lost in the Armed Forces Bowl the past two seasons, including 34-28 to Houston a year ago. Air Force had lost three straight postseason games.

Houston's bowl win last year capped Sumlin's debut season and snapped an eight-game postseason losing streak that had spanned 28 years. This time, the Cougars missed out on their first 11-win season since 1979.

After Houston was held without a touchdown before halftime, Tyron Carrier returned the opening kickoff of the second half 79 yards for his fourth TD this season. He took the ball near the left sideline, then ran to the middle of the field before shooting through a gap and running untouched to get the Cougars within 24-13.

Air Force immediately responded with its first kickoff return for a touchdown since 1985. Jonathan Warzeka fielded the ball and stepped back into the end zone before running 100 yards. Five Houston players got their hands on him but couldn't get him down.

According to STATS, it was only the sixth major college game since 1996 with kickoff return touchdowns on consecutive plays. None of them had been in a bowl game.

After the kickoff returns, Keenum threw a 10-yard TD to Patrick Edwards to make it 31-20. That gave Keenum a TD pass in 30 consecutive games , but this was the first time in that streak that he had more picks than scores.

Houston managed only 331 total yards after coming in with a nation-best 581 yards per game and averaging 44 points.

When Jefferson slipped down trying to run on third-and-goal from the 2 with 17 seconds and no timeouts left just before halftime, he quickly got the offense off the field and the kicking team got out in time for Erik Soderberg's 27-yard field goal.

"Just overall, we played terrific football today. If you want to break it down into the three phases, one by one, we really were outstanding," coach Troy Calhoun said. "Yet even above that, just the unity, the kind of team chemistry, the spirit that's part of these guys."
Copyright © 2019, The San Diego Union-Tribune
Football

2010 Air Force Falcons Coach Troy Calhoun

The 2010 season and home opener was played on Sep 5, 2010 against Northwestern State in Falcon Stadium Colorado Springs, CO. The Falcons shellacked the Demons W (65-21) before 42,236. On Sep 11, at home, the Falcons beat BYU W (35–14) before 46,692. Then, on Sep 18 at # 7 Oklahoma in Gaylord Family Oklahoma Memorial Stadium Norman, OK, the Sooners beat the Falcons L (24–27) before. 84,332

Then on Sep 25 at Wyoming's War Memorial Stadium Laramie, WY, the Falcons beat the Cowboys W (20–14) before 22,413. At Falcon stadium on Oct 2, v Navy, Air force won the first leg of the Commander-in-Chief's Trophy W (14-16) Before 47,565. On Oct 9, at home, #25 Air Force pounded Colorado State W (49–27) before 41,547. Then at San Diego State on Oct 16, in Qualcomm Stadium San Diego, CA, the Rams beat the Falcons L (25–27) before 28,178.

At #4 TCU, on Oct 23, the Horned Frogs slugged the Falcons at Amon G. Carter Stadium Fort Worth, TX L (7–38) before 46,096. Then, on October 30, the Falcons lost their next game to the #8 Utah

Utes at home L (23–28) before 37,211. Air Force came back to beat Army W (42-22) before 38128 on Nov 6 in Michie Stadium West Point, NY to wrap up the second leg and claim the Commander-in-Chief's Trophy. On Nov 13, at home, the Falcons beat the Lobos of New Mexico W (48–23) before 27,309. Then, to finish the regular season, on Nov 18, Air Force beat UNLV at Sam Boyd Stadium Whitney, NV W (35–20) before 13,790.

With eight regular season wins, the Falcons qualified for the Independence Bowl and played Georgia Tech on December 27, 2010 at 3:00 p.m. in Independence Stadium • Shreveport, LA. Air Force won in a low scoring match W (14–7) before 39,362.

2010 Independence Bowl Highlights
Falcons Are Independence Bowl Champions

https://goairforcefalcons.com/news/2010/12/27/Falcons_Are_Independence_Bowl_Champions.aspx

Dec. 27, 2010

SHREVEPORT, La. (AP) - The Independence Bowl featured the two best running teams in the nation, and special teams proved to be the unlikely difference.

Air Force cashed in when Georgia Tech muffed a punt in the second half, getting a go-ahead touchdown run from Jared Tew in a 14-7 victory Monday.

Backup kicker Zack Bell converted the first two field-goal attempts of his career before Tew's 3-yard run gave the Falcons (9-4) the lead for good. Air Force's only touchdown came four plays after Daniel McKayhan's second muffed punt of the game.

Georgia Tech's 327 yards rushing per game this season edged Air Force's 317.9 average for the nation's top spot. Both teams use a heavy dose of option, which often catches opponents off guard because it's a relatively rare offense.

But with each defense familiar with the scheme, there were no surprises, and both teams were held under their season rushing average - Georgia Tech with 279 and Air Force with 170.

Air Force's Tim Jefferson completed 11 of 23 passes for 117 yards. Bell's field goals came from 41 and 42 yards.

Georgia Tech's Tevin Washington rushed for 131 yards and Anthony Allen added 91 as Georgia Tech outgained Air Force 320-287. But the Yellow Jackets committed four turnovers - including three fumbles. Georgia Tech (6-7) came into the game hobbled by injuries, academic casualties and misbehavior.

Joshua Nesbitt, the ACC's career leading rusher for a quarterback, missed the game because of a broken right arm. Top receiver Stephen Hill and starting safety Mario Edwards were among four players declared ineligible because of various academic issues

On Sunday, the Yellow Jackets announced that three players - including defensive end Anthony Egbuniwe and defensive backs Michael Peterson and Louis Young - would miss the first half because of a curfew violation.

Even with all those issues, Georgia Tech probably would have won if not for the turnovers. Instead, the Yellow Jackets dropped their sixth consecutive bowl and posted their first losing season in 14 years.

Bell's 42-yard field goal gave Air Force the lead in the first quarter, but Georgia Tech responded with a 12-play, 69-yard drive capped by Anthony Allen's 5-yard touchdown run. The clock-chewing possession was all running plays stayed as the Yellow Jackets ran over and around the Falcons' defense.

Air Force was much more willing to take shots through the air, throwing 17 passes in the first half, but couldn't take advantage of its opportunities. Jonathan Warzeka dropped what looked to be a sure touchdown pass in the second quarter, and the Falcons couldn't convert on three fourth-down opportunities in the first half - including one that was well within field-goal range had they elected to kick. Bell's 41-yard kick as time expired in the second quarter cut Georgia Tech's lead to 7-6 at halftime.

The Yellow Jackets appeared to take control of the game in the second half, but a handful of crucial mistakes proved to be too much for them to overcome.

A nearly nine-minute drive opening the third ended when Washington fumbled on the Air Force 5. Then McKayhan's muffed punts - including the one at the Georgia Tech 14 that led to Air Force's winning touchdown - gave the Falcons terrific field position.

After Tew's scoring run, the Falcons converted the 2-point conversion on a Warzeka run.

Georgia Tech had one last chance to tie it, but a last-gasp pass toward the end zone was intercepted by Jon Davis.

2011 Air Force Falcons Coach Troy Calhoun

The 2011 season and home opener was played on September 3, 2011 at home against South Dakota in Falcon Stadium Colorado Springs, The Falcons prevailed W (37-20). At home on Sep 10, # 25 TCU beat Air Force L (19–35) before 42,107. At home on Sep 24, Air Force pounded Tennessee State W (63–24) before 33,487. Then, on Oct 1 at Navy in the Navy – Marine Corps Memorial Stadium Annapolis, MD, the Falcons won by one-point W (35-34) in OT before 37,506, for the first leg of the Commander-in-Chief's Trophy. At Notre Dame on Oct 8, in Notre Dame Stadium Notre Dame, IN, the Fighting Irish pummeled the Air Force in a shootout L (33–59) before 80,795.

At home on Oct 13, San Diego State beat Air Force L (27–41) before 27,490. #7 Boise State beat Air Force on Oct 22 in Bronco Stadium Boise, ID L (26–37) before 34,196[. On Oct 29 at New Mexico's University Stadium Albuquerque, NM, Air Force lambasted the Lobos in a big shutout W (42–0) before 16,691. At home on Nov 5, Air Force beat the Black Knights for the second and deciding leg of the Commander-in-Chief's Trophy W (24–14) before 46,709.

On Nov Wyoming beat Air Force at home in Falcon Stadium, L (17–25) before 33,823. On Nov 19, at home, Air Force pounded UNLV W (45–17) before 24,401. On Nov 26 at Colorado State in Hughes

Stadium Fort Collins, CO for the Ram–Falcon Trophy, Air Force beat the Rams in a shootout W (45–21) before 14,107

In the Military Bowl on December 28, 2011, at 2:30 p.m., Toledo beat the Air Force in RFK Stadium Washington, D.C. L (41–42) before 25,042.

2011 Military Bowl Highlights

This 2011 Military Bowl Recap is presented by the game sponsor, Northrop Grumman

http://www.northropgrumman.com/MediaResources/MediaKits/MilitaryBowl/Pages/2011.aspx

Dec. 28, 2011 — In one of the most exciting college football bowl games in recent memory, the University of Toledo Rockets held off the Air Force Academy Falcons, 42-41, in the 2011 Military Bowl.

The game was presented by Northrop Grumman at historic Robert F. Kennedy (RFK) Stadium in Washington, D.C. in front of 25,042 fans.

The game, which benefitted the USO, was televised live nationally on ESPN for the fourth straight year. Toledo's Bernard Reedy, who scored three touchdowns, was named the game's Most Valuable Player (MVP).

Northrop Grumman's Chairman, Chief Executive Officer and President Wes Bush (left), along with Vice President for Strategic Communications, Randy Belote (center), and Corporate Vice President of Communications, Darryl Fraser(right), scan the skies for the Northrop Grumman-built B-2 Spirit stealth bomber as it flies over RFK Stadium just before kickoff.

Volunteers roll out a giant American flag across the field in preparation of the 2011 Military Bowl.

The Northrop Grumman-built B-2 Spirit stealth bomber flies over RFK Stadium just before kickoff.

About the Sponsorship

The sponsorship of the game has been a very special and unique opportunity for Northrop Grumman to support the work of the USO. For decades, this organization has been there to boost the morale of our servicemen and women, at home and abroad. From entertaining the troops overseas, to establishing welcome centers across the country, to reaching out to the families of service members, the USO has long demonstrated the enduring American tradition of respect and support for our armed forces.

At Northrop Grumman, we share this tradition, working positively and creatively with the USO over many years for the benefit of service members. For example, Northrop Grumman was the first supporter of the Operation USO Care Package program, and has contributed money, resources and time to the care package program and to USO centers around the world.

Through this sponsorship of the Military Bowl, Northrop Grumman has been able to expand this relationship, delivering all net proceeds from the game to the USO. Additional information about the game can be found on the bowl's website, www.militarybowl.com.

Toledo takes Military Bowl thanks to Air Force's botched 2-point conversion
Dec 28, 2011
Associated Press

WASHINGTON -- Even the youngest head coach in the country knows not to expect the conventional from Air Force. After all, the Falcons had already scored three fourth-down touchdowns, including the one that had just tied the Military Bowl with 52 seconds to play.

So 32-year-old Matt Campbell, leading Toledo for the first time, wasn't surprised when Air Force lined up to kick the extra point and then ran a fake, going for two to win the game instead of sending it to overtime.

The Rockets were ready.

Holder David Baska got bottled up trying to run the option. The ball squirted toward kicker Parker Herrington, who chased it until it went out of bounds in the end zone, and Toledo started celebrating its 42-41 victory Wednesday night at RFK Stadium.

"We talked about it, first and foremost, because they fake some extra points and fake some field goals," said Campbell, the Toledo offensive coordinator who was promoted this month to the head job after Tim Beckman left for Illinois. "Ironically, we were in the same situation last year in our bowl game. I give credit to our staff. We got ourselves into a defensive call. We were not in a 'block' look."

Toledo succeeded in taking a one-point lead with a 2-point conversion near the end of last year's Little Caesars Pizza Bowl, but the Rockets lost the game to Florida International on a field goal on the game's final play.

This time, the wild ending to a wild game went their way in the school's first bowl win since 2005.

The game matched two of the top 25 scoring teams in the country, and they wasted little time living up to their reputations. It was Mid-American Conference member Toledo's spread offense against

Mountain West Air Force's triple option, and the idea of a huddle seemed a quaint, antiquated concept.

Back and forth they went. A kickoff return for 87 yards. A pitch around the left end for 60. Touchdown passes for 49 and 37 yards. A pair of botched onside kicks.

And that was just the first half.

Tim Jefferson, the first quarterback in service academy history to lead his team to four consecutive bowl games, completed 13 of 22 passes for 159 yards with two touchdowns and one interception for Air Force (7-6). Jonathan Warzeka had a career-best 60-yard run to set up one touchdown, and his 37-yard reception on fourth-and-3 tied the game 28-all heading into halftime.

There was even room for a defensive score: Toledo safety Jermaine Robinson's 37-yard interception runback after he corralled a tipped pass deep in the secondary.

It all came down to a gutsy decision on a 2-point conversion. It appeared that Baska tried to pitch the ball to Herrington, but Air Force coach Troy Calhoun said the ball just popped out.
Either way, the coach wasn't about to second-guess himself.

"I thought we had an excellent chance to seal and win the game right there. It didn't work out," Calhoun said. "We didn't convert it, so you better be able to live with it. We're a group that over the last six years, we're going to go for it on fourth down if we think there are chances we can take. When we have a pretty darn good opportunity to convert one, we're going to do it. That's the way we're going to play."

2012 Air Force Falcons Coach Troy Calhoun

The 2012 season and home opener was played on September 1, 2012 at home against Idaho State in Falcon Stadium Colorado Springs, The Falcons pummeled the Bengals W (49-21) before 35,282. At home on Sep 8, # 19 Michigan beat Air Force L (25-31)in Michigan Stadium • Ann Arbor, MI before a *Big-House* crowd of 112,522. At UNLV on

Sep 22 in Sam Boyd Stadium Whitney, NV, The Falcons prevailed L (35–38) before 14,054. Then, on Sep 29 at home, for the Ram-Falcon Trophy, the Falcons beat Colorado State W (42–21) before 38,562.

At home on Oct 6 Navy beat Air Force L (21-28) before 38,927 for the first leg of the Commander-in-Chief's Trophy. On Oct 13 at Wyoming's War Memorial Stadium Laramie, WY, the Falcons nosed out the Cowboys W (28–27) before 22,627. Then, on Oct 20 at home, the Air Force beat the Lobos of New Mexico W (28–23) before 29,726 On Oct 26 at home, the Falcons defeated Nevada W (48–31) before 24,277.

On Nov 3 at Army's Michie Stadium West Point, NY the Black Knights beat the Falcons L 21–41 before 37,707. Navy won the Commander-in-Chief's Trophy in 2012. On Nov 10 at San Diego State in Qualcomm Stadium San Diego, CA, the Aztecs beat the Falcons L (9–28) before 30,266. Then, on Nov 16, Air Force beat Hawaii at home W (21–7) before 25,213. At Fresno State on Nov 24 in Bulldog Stadium Fresno, CA, Air Force was squashed L (15–48) before 36,240 in the final game of the regular season.

On December 29, 2012, at 9:45 a.m., Rice beat Airforce L (14-33) in Amon G. Carter Stadium Fort Worth, TX in the Armed Forces Bowl before 40,754.

Highlights of the Armed Services Bowl 2012

Academy falls to Rice in Armed Forces Bowl
By John Van Winkle, Air Force Academy Public Affairs /
Published **December 30, 2012**

2012 ARMED FORCES BOWL
Academy fell 33-14 to Rice University

Rice running back Charles Ross is dragged down during the 2012 Armed Forces Bowl by a host of falcon defenders, including defensive backs Brian Lindsay, bottom, and Chris Miller, right. The bowl game was held December 28 in Ft. Worth, Texas. (U.S. Air Force photo/Sarah Chambers)

Academy falls to Rice in Armed Forces Bowl
By John Van Winkle, Air Force Academy Public Affairs / Published December 30, 2012

Above pic shows Rice running back Charles Ross being dragged down during the 2012 Armed Forces Bowl by a host of falcon defenders, including defensive backs Brian Lindsay, bottom, and Chris Miller, right.

The bowl game was held December 28 in Ft. Worth, Texas. (U.S. Air Force photo/Sarah Chambers)

FORT WORTH, Texas (AFNS) -- The Air Force Academy fell 14-33 to Rice University in the 2012 Armed Forces Bowl today.

Rice University used a combination of size, speed and better execution to dominate the second half and end the Falcons season with a loss.

After a few initial three-and-outs, Rice mounted its first sustained drive to score when quarterback Taylor McHargue connected with receiver Jordan Taylor from 16-yards out in the corner of the end zone to go up 7-0.

McHargue would later go with a concussion and not return. Air Force also switched out under center, pulling senior quarterback Connor Dietz in the second quarter in favor of sophomore Kale Pearson, hoping to spark an offense that can stay on the field for more than three consecutive plays.

"We came into the game expecting both guys to play for us at quarterback," said Falcons head coach Troy Calhoun. "Kale played well for us in the second quarter."

Pearson commanded the Falcons' first sustained drive of the game and ended the series with a 9-yard run around the right to tie the game at 7-all. The Falcons took the lead a few series later when senior running back Wes Cobb dove in from a yard out for the Falcons' second touchdown.

Kicker Parker Herrington added the extra point, giving the Falcons a 14-7 lead. The Owls evened the score before the half and took control of the game from that point on, keeping the Falcons out of the end zone and on their heels for the remainder of the game. Rice would score four times in the second half to mount and sustain a 33-14 lead until time ran out.

"At every single spot, we didn't play well enough in the second half to win a game," said Calhoun.

On offense, the Falcons would end the day converting only four of 14 third downs, and one of two on fourth down. Two critical turnovers in the fourth quarter also killed any chance the Falcons had of mounting a comeback.

"We put an awful lot of strain on our defense," said Calhoun. "Sometimes it was in field position, and sometimes it wasn't getting enough first downs. Sometimes it was in third downs for the other team. When your opponent has 20 third downs, you aren't stopping them enough to give your offense a shot."

Defensively, the Falcons allowed 503 yards of offense to sustain several long drives and win time of possession battle by over 15 minutes.

"It just came down to execution," said senior linebacker Austin Niklas, Air Force's move valuable player for the game.

Size was also an advantage that Rice monopolized. It is an advantage that most opponents have over service academy football teams. Service academy teams compensate for this up front with their triple-option offenses, and utilize technique, strength and mobility to overcome the opponents' mass advantage.

But against Rice's offense and their three wide-receiver set, the Falcons smaller secondary spent the game in their opponent's shadows. Between Rice's two quarterbacks, the Falcons gave up 295 yards in passing offense and had zero interceptions.

"It was a combo of our secondary, our defensive backs, getting beat up, and our pass rush. Rice has a lot better size on the ends and our pass rush just didn't bring it home," said senior linebacker Alex Means.

Rice receiver Jordan Taylor used his 6'5" frame to tower over Falcon defenders and score all three of Rice's touchdowns.

"I wish we had won," said Niklas. "We fought hard the whole game. Rice has a good football team, and we were unable to stop them consistently in the second half. The Bell Helicopter Armed Forces Bowl people were great, and we appreciated our time here."

For the Falcons, this concludes their 2012 college football season. After a few more days of holiday leave, next up for the players will be off-season workouts in the weight room in January for the underclassmen. For most of the 22 seniors, it' was the last game of their collegiate careers, so they just had one more semester and graduation awaiting them. For the coaches, recruiting trips and recruiting visits will take the forefront of the days to come, as well as preparations for spring football in early 2013.

2013 Air Force Falcons Coach Troy Calhoun

This was the first really poor season for the Troy Calhoun Falcons. The Air Force record was 2-10; 0-8 in the Mountain West Conference. They finished in last place in the MWC.

They won no games in the Conference this year. It was as if a big spray came over the AFA football this year and it brought the Can't Play disease. It was the worst AFA results since Santa Claus first appeared before the world was born. It was not a happy year.

The 2013 season and home opener was played on August 31, 2013 at home against Colgate in Falcon Stadium Colorado Springs, The Falcons soundly defeated the Red Raiders W (38-13) before 32019. On Sep 7 at home Utah State pounded Air Force L (20–52) before 32,716. At Boise State on Sep 13 in Bronco Stadium Boise, Idaho, the Broncos walloped the Falcons. L (20–42) before 36,069. Then, on Sep 21,at home, Wyoming crushed Air Force L (23–56) before 35,389. Then on Sep 28, Nevada nosed out Air Force in shootout in Mackay Stadium Reno, Nevada L (42–45) before 24,545.

At Navy on Oct 5 in Navy–Marine Corps Memorial Stadium Annapolis, Maryland for the first leg of the Commander-in-Chief's Trophy, Navy triumphed L (10–28) before 38,225. On Oct 10 at home,

San Diego State edged out the Falcons L (20–27) before 17,280. Then, on Oct 26 at home Notre Dame slammed Air Force L (10–45) before 44,672. At home again against Army. The Falcons overpowered the Black Knights on Nov 2 W (42-28) before 36,512. Navy picked up the Commander-in-Chief's Trophy this year.

On Nov 8 at New Mexico in University Stadium Albuquerque, New Mexico, the Lobos edged out the Falcons L 37–45 before 21,833. On Nov 21, UNLV got the best of Air Force at home L (21–41) before 29,898. On Nov 30, at Colorado State in Hughes Stadium Fort Collins, Colorado in the Battle for the Ram–Falcon Trophy, the Rams got it this year for sure with a walloping L (13–58) before 15,546. And, folks for the first time in this book, I am pleased to say…"And that's all she wrote!"

2014 Air Force Falcons Coach Troy Calhoun

The Air Force record this year was very good. It was 10-3; 5-3 in the Mountain West Conference. They finished in fourth place in the MWC. They were invited to the Famous Idaho Potato Bowl where they defeated Western Michigan. How's that for a recovery?

The 2014 season and home opener was played on August 30, 2014 at home against Nicholls State in Falcon Stadium Colorado Springs, The Falcons soundly defeated the Colonels W (44-16) before 32038. At Wyoming on Sep 6 at War Memorial Stadium Laramie, WY, , the Air Force lost the contest L (13–17) before 21,246. Spreading its wings across the nation on Sep 13 at Georgia State in a game played in the Georgia Dome Atlanta, GA, the Falcons beat the Panthers W (48–38) before 16,836. Then, on Sep 27, at home, the Air Force beat Boise State W (28–14) before 30,012.

On Oct 4, which happens to be my wedding anniversary, Air Force beat Navy at home, for the first leg of the Commander-in-Chief's Trophy, W (30–21) before 37,731. On Oct 11at Utah State in Romney Stadium Logan, UT, the Falcons were defeated L (16–34) before 24,037. At home on Oct 18, the Falcons defeated New Mexico in a close match W (35–31) before 25,017.

On Nov 1 at Army in Michie Stadium West Point, NY, Air Force won the Commander-in-Chief's Trophy with this victory over Army W)23–

6) before 40,479. On Nov 8 at UNLV in Sam Boyd Stadium Whitney, NV, Air Force prevailed W (48–21) before 13,481. Against Nevada on Nov 15 at home, in Falcon Stadium, the Air Force prevailed in a semi-shootout W (45–38) in OT before 11,519. At San Diego State, on Nov 21, in Qualcomm Stadium San Diego, CA, the Aztecs beat the Falcons L (14–30) before. 28,626. Then, on Nov 28, at home, Air Force defeated # 21 Colorado State in a close match W (27–24) before 32,650.

In the famous Idaho Potato Bowl, on Dec 20 vs. Western Michigan in Albertsons Stadium Boise, ID , the Air Force prevailed W (38–24) before 18,223

Bowl Bits: Air Force 38, Western Michigan 24 (Idaho Potato Bowl)

https://www.cbssports.com/college-football/news/bowl-bits-air-force-38-western-michigan-24-idaho-potato-bowl/

Shayne Davern ran for 101 yards and two touchdowns against Western Michigan. (USATSI)

Thanks you to cbssports.com

Air Force won 10 games for the first time under Troy Calhoun after beating Western Michigan in the Famous Idaho Potato Bowl.
by Chip Patterson   @Chip_Patterson
Dec 20, 2014

Air Force and Western Michigan were two of the best turnaround stories in 2014, but it was the Falcons that were able to finish the year with a victory after a 38-24 win against Western Michigan in the Idaho Potato Bowl. The bowl victory, Air Force's first since 2010, wraps the program's first 10-win season under Troy Calhoun and gives the MW's Mountain Division three 10-win teams (Boise State and Colorado State, and both teams lost to the Falcons).

Story of the game: Jarvion Franklin made history as the first player in MAC history to be named Freshman of the Year and Offensive Player of the Year in the same season. But he was tough to find on Saturday thanks to a noted effort by Air Force to shut down the Western Michigan running attack. With eight, even nine players crowded near the line of scrimmage, the Falcons forced quarterback Zach Terrell to try and beat them through the air in cold and rainy Boise conditions. WMU wide receiver Corey Davis was the benefactor of this game plan, pulling in 8 catches for 176 yards and three touchdowns.

Meanwhile, Air Force's offense was right at home in Boise State's stadium, holding the ball for long drives thanks to a fierce commitment to the ground game. At was a slow and steady approach, but the 284-79 advantage in team rushing yards stands out more than any stat from the game.

Player of the game: Air Force linebacker Weston Steelhammer led the Falcons defense with 10 solo tackles. Some of Steelhammer's finest work this season has been done in the open field, and while the entire defense deserves this award there is only one Steelhammer.

2015 Air Force Falcons Coach Troy Calhoun

The 2015 season and home opener was played on September 5, 2015 at home against Morgan State in Falcon Stadium Colorado Springs, The Falcons walloped the Bears W (63-7) in a blowout before 33,734. On Sep 12 at home, the Falcons beat San Jose State W (37–16) before 22,389. At #4 Michigan State, the Falcons lost in Spartan Stadium

East Lansing, MI L (21–35) before 74,211. On Oct 3 at Navy's Navy-Marine Corps Memorial Stadium Annapolis, MD for the first leg of the Commander-in-Chief's Trophy, the Midshipmen defeated the Falcons L (11–33) before 32,705.

On Oct 10 at home, the Falcons defeated Wyoming in Falcon Stadium, W (31–17) before 22,023. In the Ram-Falcon Trophy game on Oct 17, Colorado State beat the Falcons in Hughes Stadium, Fort Collins, CO L (23–38(before 32,546. On Oct24 at home, the Falcons beat Fresno State W (42–14) before 20,213. Then, at Hawaii on Oct 31 in Aloha Stadium Honolulu, HI for the Kuter Trophy. The Falcons pounded the Rainbow Warriors W (58–7) before 22,430. On Nov 7 at home. Army beat the Falcons W (20-3 before 37,716r-and Navy won the 2015 Commander-in-Chief's Trophy)

On Nov 14, Air Force beat Utah State in Falcon Stadium W (35–28) before 20,083. At Boise State on Nov 20, in Albertsons Stadium Boise, ID, Air Force prevailed W (37–30) before 30,332. On Nov 28 at New Mexico's University Stadium, Albuquerque, NM, the Lobos beat the Falcons L (35–47) before 18,868

On Dec 5 in the MWC Champion-ship Game, at San Diego State's Qualcomm Stadium San Diego, CA, the Aztecs edged out the Falcons L 24–27 before 20,950.

On December 29 at 12:00 p.m. California beat Air Force at Amon G. Carter Stadium Fort Worth, TX in the shootout at the Armed Forces Bowl L (36–55) before 38,915

Highlights 2015 Armed Services Bowl

by Charles Rahrig V 3 years ago Follow @c_rahrig

Comment: The California Golden Bears and quarterback Jared Goff rolled to a win over the Air Force Falcons.

California Golden Bears 55

Air Force Falcons 36

The Armed Forces Bowl might have been a blowout, but both the California Golden Bears and Air Force Falcons put on a show. Both teams put up a lot of points on the board and it was a day where defenses were non-existent.

For California quarterback Jared Goff, it was the final game of his collegiate career. Goff headed off to the NFL Draft, where he was one of the top quarterbacks taken in the draft, if not the top quarterback off the board. He played for the Rams v Patriots in Super Bowl LIII.

He put on an impressive showing all day for the Golden Bears in this bowl game. Goff put the ball in the right spot and consistently set up his wide receivers to score touchdowns.

Air Force got the scoring fest started on the day, when Jacobi Owens ran in from a yard out to put Air Force on top. California would answer right back with a rushing touchdown of their own, as Vic Enwere also ran in from a yard out.

From there, both teams would match each other with passing touchdowns, to make it a 14-14 game. California would then begin to gain separation from Air Force.

The Golden Bears would score on three straight possessions, all of which were beautiful touchdown passes from Jared Goff. Air Force would get a score of their own in, but by then Goff and the Golden Bears had a commanding 35-21 lead at the half.

California would continue to extend their lead right out of the half, as Goff found Darius Powe for 12 yards and a touchdown. Air Force would then have a big fumble, which set up a California field goal. The game was suddenly 45-21 in favor of California and looking like a blowout.

Air Force would try to climb back in it, as Karson Roberts and Timothy McVey connected on a 57-yard score. California would respond to Air Force's touchdown to keep their big lead, when Goff continued to roll with his pass to Kenny Lawler, who made a beautiful sprint to the end zone, which gave Goff six touchdowns on the day.

The Golden Bears held a 52-29 lead and the game was all but over, save for Air Force scoring on another touchdown pass from Roberts. With time running down and a 52-36 lead, California just worked on the clock and making Air Force burn their timeouts.

California capped off their day with a field goal, to make it 55-36. With the win, California became the 2015 Armed Forces Bowl winners.

2016 Air Force Falcons Coach Troy Calhoun

The 2016 season and home opener was played on September 3, 2016 at home against Abilene Christian in Falcon Stadium Colorado Springs, The Falcons defeated the Wildcats W (37-21) before 34,128. At home on Sep 10, the Falcons pounded Georgia State's Panthers W (48–14) before 24,173. On Sep 24 at Utah State in Maverik Stadium Logan, UT, the Falcons beat the Aggies W (27–20) before 23,104. On Oct 1 at home, the Air Force beat the Navy for this leg of the Commander-in-Chief's Trophy W (28–14) before 43,063.

At Wyoming on Oct 8 in War Memorial Stadium Laramie, WY, the Cowboys beat the Falcons L (26–35) before 26,623. In Cotton Bowl Stadium on Oct 15, New Mexico beat the Air Force in Dallas, TX L (40–45) before 18,756. At home on Oct 22, Hawaii beat Air Force L

(27-34 in 2 OT periods before 29,132. After losing three games in a row, the Falcons got in gear and started on the road to a fine 10-3 season. At Fresno State on Oct 28 in Bulldog Stadium Fresno, CA, the Falcons beat the Bulldogs W 31–21 before 25,197.

On Nov 5, the Air Force beat Army in Michie Stadium West Point, NY W (31-12) before 38,443 and they won the Commander-in-Chief's Trophy. On Nov 12 at home the Falcons edged out Colorado State W 49–46 in a shootout before 23,467. On Nov 19 in another close match Air Force at San Jose State, the Falcons prevailed in San Jose, CA (41–38) before 15,533. In the season finale on Nov 25, at home, Air Force defeated # 20 Boise State 0 Boise State W (27–20) before 23,556

In the Arizona Bowl, on December 30, 2016, at 3:30 p.m., Air Force defeated South Alabama in Arizona Stadium Tucson, AZ W (45–21) before 33,868

2016 Arizona Bowl Highlights

by Connor Muldowney2 years ago Follow @connormuldowney
Thank you Connor.

COMMENT: Take a look at the highlights, final score and more from Friday evening's Arizona Bowl between South Alabama and Air Force.

SOUTH ALABAMAJAGUARS 21

AIR FORCEFALCONS 45

South Alabama opened the 2016 season with one of the best upsets of the year, beating Mississippi State on the road. The Jaguars weren't quite the same after that, as the expectations from that point on were a little unrealistic and they finished eighth in the Sun Belt with a 6-6 overall record.

Facing the potent rushing attack of Air Force on Friday evening, the Jaguars looked to make a name for themselves. However, the Falcons posed a serious problem for the 98th-ranked rushing defense. They have averaged over 300 yards per game on the season.

The Jaguars got off to a quick start, scoring two touchdowns in the first quarter and taking a 14-3 lead. It was looking like it'd be all South Alabama through the first 20 minutes as the Jaguars added another touchdown on a Dallas Davis run and the sophomore was having a big game.

Air Force stormed back, scoring 42 straight points and just wearing down the Jaguars' defense. The Falcons' rushing attack was doing damage and the second half was all theirs. Air Force was owning the trenches and it was clear who the stronger team was.

All the Falcons had to do in the fourth was run out the clock, winning big.

Chapter 12 Coach Troy Calhoun 2017-2018

Calhoun   Coach # 7

Year	Coach	Record	Conference Record
2017	Troy Calhoun	5–7	4–4
2018	Troy Calhoun	5–7	3–5

2017 Air Force Falcons Coach Troy Calhoun

The 2017 season and home opener was played on September 2, 2017 at home against VMI in Falcon Stadium Colorado Springs, The Falcons shellacked the Keydets in a shutout W (62-0) before 37,286. On Sep #7 Michigan beat Air Force in Michigan Stadium (The Big House) Ann Arbor, MI L 13–29 before 111,387. On Sep 23, at home #22 San Diego State beat the Air force L 24–28 before 27,575. Then, on Sep 30 at New Mexico's Dreamstyle Stadium Albuquerque, NM, the Lobos beat the Falcons L (38–56) before 21,864

On October 7, Navy beat Air Force at Navy–Marine Corps Memorial Stadium Annapolis, MD for the first leg of the Commander-in-Chief's

Trophy L (45–48) before 38,792. On Oct 14, at home, the Air Force defeated UNLV in a close match W (34–30) before 26,679. At Nevada on Oct 20 in Mackay Stadium Reno, NV, the Falcons prevailed in a really close shootout W 45–42 before, 16,789. Then, on Oct 28 at Colorado State, the Falcons beat the Rams W 45–28 before 33,074. Then, on Nov 4 at home, in the second leg of the Commander-in-Chief's Trophy, Army shut-out the Air Force L (0–21) before 41,875

On Nov 11 at home, Wyoming beat the Falcons L (14–28) before 24,257. At Boise State, on Nov 18, at Albertsons Stadium Boise, ID, the Broncos beat the Falcons L (19–44) before 33,030. In the final game of the 2017 season at home, on Nov 25 The Air Force edged out Utah State W (38–35) before 17,252

2018 Air Force Falcons Coach Troy Calhoun

During the Mountain West media days held July 24–25 at the Cosmopolitan on the Las Vegas Strip, the Falcons were predicted to finish in fifth place in the Mountain Division. The prognosticators were right. Air Force did not have any players selected to the preseason all-Mountain West team. Expectations were quite low for the season.

The 2018 season and home opener was played on September 1, 2018 at home against #20 FCS Stony Brook in Falcon Stadium Colorado Springs, The Falcons pounded the Seawolves in a shutout W (38-0) before 33,415. At Florida Atlantic on Sep 8 in FAU Stadium in Boca Raton, FL, the Owls defeated the Falcons L (27–33) before 24,101. Then, on Sep 22 Utah State defeated the Falcons in Maverik Stadium Logan, UT, L (32–42) before 22,720. On Sep 29, Nevada edged out the Falcons at home at Falcon Stadium L (25–28) before 23,707.

On Oct 6, at home, the Falcons pounded Navy for the first leg of the Commander-in-Chief's Trophy, W (35–7) before 40,175. At San Diego State on Oct 12, in SDCCU Stadium San Diego, CA, the Falcons were edged out of a victory over the Aztecs L (17–21) before 25,326. At UNLV, on Oct 19 in Sam Boyd Stadium Whitney, NV, the Falcons got the victory 41–35 before 17,881. Then, on Oct 27, at home, Boise State got the best of the Falcons L (38–48) before 27,753.

At Army's Michie Stadium West Point, NY for the second leg of the Commander-in-Chief's Trophy, the Black Knights defeated the

Falcons L (14–17) before 38,502. Army won the Trophy for the second-year in a row. At home on Nov 10, the Falcons defeated the New Mexico Lobos W (42–24) before 23,723.

Then, as the season was winding down, on Nov 17 at Wyoming's War Memorial Stadium Laramie, WY, the Cowboys defeated the Falcons L (27–35) before 14,966. On Nov 22 at home, the Falcons defeated Colorado State in Falcon Stadium, W (27–19) before 17,432

Troy Calhoun Wrap Up –Waiting for 2019

Like you, I love America and I love what all the AFA heroes have done for all Americans.

David Ramsey: Troy Calhoun must build Air Force football winner in 2019, or else
By: David Ramsey

Nov 26, 2018

Troy Calhoun stands in the same dangerous position where Ben Martin and Fisher DeBerry once stood.

Calhoun has performed wonders in his dozen seasons as Air Force football coach. He's earned 87 victories along with eight winning seasons and nine bowl trips. He immediately revived a fallen program when he arrived in 2007.

Remember, Martin and DeBerry performed wonders with the Falcons, too. Both flirted with unbeaten seasons and national championships. Both were blessed with magical offensive minds. Both are legends, a vastly overused word, but both men deserve the description.

SPORTS COVERAGE

Air Force's investment in young roster could pay dividends in upcoming football seasons by Brent Briggeman

> Both departed Air Force after fumbling their magic. Martin departed in 1977 after four straight losing seasons. DeBerry resigned in 2006 after three straight losing seasons.
>
> Calhoun oversees a broken program that has lost 14 of 22 Football Bowl Subdivision games. From 2007 to 2010, Calhoun won 34 of 52 games and looked ready to build a regional, if not quite national, power. Since then, he's dropped 48 of 93 FBS games with four losing seasons. (DeBerry stumbled to two losing records in his first 20 seasons.)
>
> The Falcons crawled to four FBS victories this season, and none were dazzling. Teams that lost to the Falcons — CSU, New Mexico, UNLV and Navy – lost 35 of 48 games in 2018. Calhoun declined a request to explain his plans to repair the Falcons.
>
> This is no surprise.
>
> For years, dating to 2012 or so, he's declined to speak clearly, or even kind of clearly, about his team. He instead speaks in mystifying sentences, but mystifying everyone is central to a strategy only he comprehends.

He refuses to explain his team to fans. He declines to reveal how deeply he cares for his players and winning at his alma mater. Calhoun is not, in his media moments, exposing who he really is. In his first few seasons with the Falcons, Calhoun was open and funny and honest. That's the real Calhoun, the man his friends know, the man hidden beneath a strange façade of his own construction.

His waste-everybody's-time media strategy is a mistake and one reason so many seats are empty on Saturdays at Falcon Stadium. His say-nothing media approach is universally unpopular, and administrators, faculty, cadets, athletes and coaches at the Air Force Academy are included in this realm of universal unpopularity. But Calhoun's misguided, failed media strategy will not end his days as Air Force coach. He can keep talking weird for another decade, as long as he rediscovers how to win.

Losing ends coaching careers. This truth crashed into the lives of Martin and DeBerry, both noble men. This truth currently stares at Calhoun.

Calhoun's prime problem is defensive weakness, a problem that has dogged the program for much of the 21st century. The 2018 Falcons averaged 30.2 points, enough for a winning record, especially with their weak schedule.

Looked at from one angle, the 2018 defense took a big jump from 2017. The nation's worst run defense became stout against the rush, and the Falcons surrendered 80 fewer points.

But when it mattered most, the defense seldom delivered. The 2017 team allowed 33 or more points five times. So did the 2018 defense, and the Falcons lost four of those five. Fierce and wise defending could have turned gloomy 5-7 to (somewhat) uplifting 7-5.

Defense wasn't the lone problem. Lack of nerve in play calling doomed the Falcons to defeats against Army and Wyoming, the bitterest afternoons of 2018. When imagination was required to seize victory, imagination seldom was seen.

Reason remains for optimism. The Falcons are young and junior-to-be quarterback Donald Hammond III has the look of a program-

lifting star. (I thought the same thing about junior-to-be QB Arion Worthman two years ago.) Calhoun supporters can talk, with some weight, about a winner just around the bend.

That was the talk a year ago, too, and Calhoun and his Falcons failed to deliver. A lost team wandered, once again, to a losing record. Calhoun deserves patience. I get that.

The patience tank runs perilously low with empty within sight.

That's all for now folks!

We hope to bring out another version of Great Coaches in Air Force Football in about five years. It will have a nice section on Air Force Academy Football that offers a commentary on what's new

Thank you for choosing this book among the many that are in your options list. I sincerely appreciate it! This is the third of three new Air Force books that have been released since February 1.

The best to you all – Go Air Force!

Other Books by Brian Kelly: (amazon.com, and Kindle)

<u>Great Moments in Air Force Football</u>. From the first game to the current season.
<u>The Ghost of Wilkes-Barre Future</u> A prescription for making the city a success.
<u>Great Coaches in Navy Football</u>: From Coach 1 to Coach #39 Ken Niumatalolo
<u>Great Moments in Navy Football</u>: From the beginning of football to the 2018 Seasonl
<u>Great Players in Navy Football</u>: From the first player to the Current Seasons
<u>No Tree! No Toys! No Toot Toot!</u> Heartwarming story. Christmas disappeared while 19 month old was napping
<u>How to End DACA, Sanctuary Cities, & Resident Illegal Aliens</u> . best solution to wipe shadows in America.
<u>Government Must Stop Ripping Off Seniors' Social Security!</u>: Hey buddy, seniors can no longer spare a dime?
<u>Special Report: Solving America's Student Debt Crisis!</u>: The only real solution to the $1.52 Trillion debt
<u>How to End DACA, Sanctuary Cities, & Resident Illegal Aliens</u> . best solution to wipe shadows in America.
<u>The Winning Political Platform for America</u> Unique winning approach to solve the big problems in America.
<u>Lou Barletta v Bob Casey for US Senate</u>   Barletta's unique approach to solving the big problems in America.
<u>John Chrin v Matt Cartwright for Congress</u> Chrin has a unique approach to solving big problems in America.
<u>The Cure for Hate !!!</u> Can the cure be any worse than this disease that is crippling America?
<u>Andrew Cuomo's Time to Go?</u> "He Was Never that Great!": Cuomo says America never that great
<u>White People Are Bad! Bad! Bad!</u> Whoever thought a popular slogan in 2018 would be It's OK to be White!
<u>The Fake News Media Is Also Corrupt !!!</u>: Fake press / media today is not worthy to be 4th Estate.
<u>God Gave US Donald Trump?</u>   Trump was sent from God as the people's answer
<u>Millennials Say America Was "Never That Great"</u>: Too many pleased days of political chumps not over!
<u>White People Are Bad! Bad! Bad!</u> In 2018, too many people find race as a non-equalizer.
<u>It's Time for The John Doe Party</u>… Don't you think? By By Elephants.
<u>Great Players in Florida Gators Football</u>… Tim Tebow and a ton of other great players
<u>Great Coaches in Florida Gators Football</u>… The best coaches in Gator history.
<u>The Constitution by Hamilton, Jefferson, Madison, et al</u>. The Real Constitution
<u>The Constitution Companion.</u> Will help you learn and understand the Constitution
<u>Great Coaches in Clemson Football</u> The best Clemson Coaches right to Dabo Swinney
<u>Great Players in Clemson Football</u> The best Clemson players in history
<u>Winning Back America.</u> America's been stolen and can be won back completely
<u>The Founding of America…</u> Great book to pick up a lot of great facts
<u>Defeating America's Career Politicians</u>. The scoundrels need to go.
<u>Midnight Mass by Jack Lammers</u>… You remember what it was like Great story
<u>The Bike by Jack Lammers</u>… Great heartwarming Story by Jack
<u>Wipe Out All Student Loan Debt</u>--Now! Watch the economy go boom!
<u>No Free Lunch Pay Back Welfare!</u> Why not pay it back?
<u>Deport All Millennials Now!!!</u> Why they deserve to be deported and/or saved
<u>DELETE the EPA, Please!</u> The worst decisions to hurt America
<u>Taxation Without Representation</u> 4th Edition Should we throw the TEA overboard again?
<u>Four Great Political Essays by Thomas Dawson</u>
<u>Top Ten Political Books for 2018</u>… Cliffnotes Version of 10 Political Books
<u>Top Six Patriotic Books for 2018</u>… Cliffnotes version of 6 Patriotic Boosk
<u>Why Trump Got Elected!</u>.. It's great to hear about a great milestone in America!
<u>The Day the Free Press Died</u>. Corrupt Press Lives on!
<u>Solved</u> (Immigration) The best solutions for 2018
<u>Solved II</u> (Obamacare, Social Security, Student Debt) Check it out; They're solved.
<u>Great Moments in Pittsburgh Steelers Football</u>... Six Super Bowls and more.
<u>Great Players in Pittsburgh Steelers Football</u> ,,,Chuck Noll, Bill Cowher, Mike Tomin, etc.
<u>Great Coaches in New England Patriots Football</u>,,, Bill Belichick the one and only plus others
<u>Great Players in New England Patriots Football</u>… Tom Brady, Drew Bledsoe et al.
<u>Great Coaches in Philadelphia Eagles Football</u>..Andy Reid, Doug Pederson & Lots more
<u>Great Players in Philadelphia Eagles Football</u> Great players such as Sonny Jurgenson
<u>Great Coaches in Syracuse Football</u> All the greats including Ben Schwartzwalder
<u>Great Players in Syracuse Football</u>. Highlights best players such as Jim Brown & Donovan McNabb
<u>Millennials are People Too !!!</u> Give US millennials help to live American Dream
<u>Brian Kelly for the United States Senate from PA</u>: Fresh Face for US Senate
<u>The Candidate's Bible</u>. Don't pray for your campaign without this bible
<u>Rush Limbaugh's Platform for Americans</u>… Rush will love it
<u>Sean Hannity's Platform for Americans</u>… Sean will love it
<u>Donald Trump's New Platform for Americans.</u> Make Trump unbeatable in 2020
<u>Tariffs Are Good for America!</u> One of the best tools a president can have
<u>Great Coaches in Pittsburgh Steelers Football</u> Sixteen of the best coaches ever to coach in pro football.
<u>Great Moments in New England Patriots Football</u> Great football moments from Boston to New England
<u>Great Moments in Philadelphia Eagles Football.</u> The best from the Eagles from the beginning of football.
<u>Great Moments in Syracuse Football</u> The great moments, coaches & players in Syracuse Football
<u>Boost Social Security Now!</u> Hey Buddy Can You Spare a Dime?
<u>The Birth of American Football.</u> From the first college game in 1869 to the last Super Bowl

Obamacare: A One-Line Repeal Congress must get this done.
A Wilkes-Barre Christmas Story A wonderful town makes Christmas all the better
A Boy, A Bike, A Train, and a Christmas Miracle A Christmas story that will melt your heart
Pay-to-Go America-First Immigration Fix
Legalizing Illegal Aliens Via Resident Visas Americans-first plan saves $Trillions. Learn how!
60 Million Illegal Aliens in America!!! A simple, America-first solution.
The Bill of Rights By Founder James Madison Refresh *your knowledge of the specific rights for all*
Great Players in Army Football Great Army Football played by great players..
Great Coaches in Army Football Army's coaches are all great.
Great Moments in Army Football Army Football at its best.
Great Moments in Florida Gators Football Gators Football from the start. This is the book.
Great Moments in Clemson Football CU Football at its best. This is the book.
Great Moments in Florida Gators Football Gators Football from the start. This is the book.
The Constitution Companion. A Guide to Reading and Comprehending the Constitution
The Constitution by Hamilton, Jefferson, & Madison – Big type and in English
PATERNO: The Dark Days After Win # 409. Sky began to fall within days of win # 409.
JoePa 409 Victories: Say No More! Winningest Division I-A football coach ever
American College Football: The Beginning From before day one football was played.
Great Coaches in Alabama Football Challenging the coaches of every other program!
Great Coaches in Penn State Football the Best Coaches in PSU's football program
Great Players in Penn State Football The best players in PSU's football program
Great Players in Notre Dame Football The best players in ND's football program
Great Coaches in Notre Dame Football The best coaches in any football program
Great Players in Alabama Football from Quarterbacks to offensive Linemen Greats!
Great Moments in Alabama Football AU Football from the start. This is the book.
Great Moments in Penn State Football PSU Football, start--games, coaches, players,
Great Moments in Notre Dame Football ND Football, start, games, coaches, players
Cross Country with the Parents A great trip from East Coast to West with the kids
Seniors, Social Security & the Minimum Wage. Things seniors need to know.
How to Write Your First Book and Publish It with CreateSpace. You too can be an author.
The US Immigration Fix--It's all in here. Finally, an answer.
I had a Dream IBM Could be #1 Again The title is self-explanatory
WineDiets.Com Presents The Wine Diet Learn how to lose weight while having fun.
Wilkes-Barre, PA; Return to Glory Wilkes-Barre City's return to glory
Geoffrey Parsons' Epoch... The Land of Fair Play Better than the original.
The Bill of Rights 4 Dummmies! This is the best book to learn about your rights.
Sol Bloom's Epoch ...Story of the Constitution The best book to learn the Constitution
America 4 Dummmies! All Americans should read to learn about this great country.
The Electoral College 4 Dummmies! How does it really work?
The All-Everything Machine Story about IBM's finest computer server.
ThankYou IBM! This book explains how IBM was beaten in the computer marketplace by neophytes

Amazon.com/author/brianwkelly
Brian W. Kelly has written 193 books.
Thank you for buying this one.
Other Kelly books can be found at amazon.com/author/brianwkelly